MOON

52 THINGS TO DO IN
NASHVILLE

MARGARET LITTMAN

CONTENTS

Day Trips and Getaways

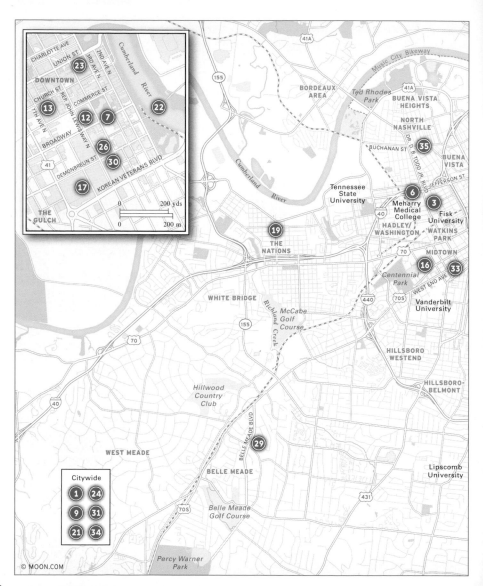

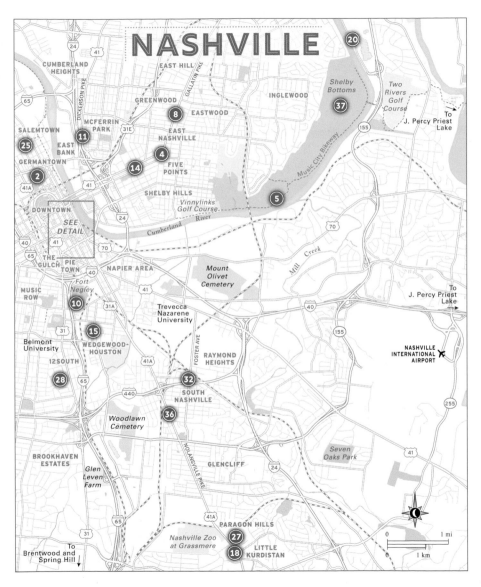

NASHVILLE

CUMBERLAND
HEIGHTS

EAST HILL

GREENWOOD

EASTWOOD

INGLEWOOD

Shelby
Bottoms

Two
Rivers
Golf
Course

To
J. Percy Priest
Lake

McFERRIN
PARK

EAST
NASHVILLE

FIVE
POINTS

SALEMTOWN

EAST
BANK

GERMANTOWN

SHELBY HILLS

Vinnylinks
Golf Course

Cumberland River

DOWNTOWN

SEE
DETAIL

THE
GULCH

PIE
TOWN

NAPIER AREA

Mount
Olivet
Cemetery

Mill Creek

To
J. Percy Priest
Lake

MUSIC
ROW

Fort
Negley

Trevecca
Nazarene
University

NASHVILLE
INTERNATIONAL
AIRPORT

Belmont
University

WEDGEWOOD-
HOUSTON

RAYMOND
HEIGHTS

12SOUTH

SOUTH
NASHVILLE

BROOKHAVEN
ESTATES

Glen
Leven
Farm

Woodlawn
Cemetery

GLENCLIFF

Seven
Oaks
Park

To
Brentwood and
Spring Hill

Nashville Zoo
at Grassmere

PARAGON HILLS

LITTLE
KURDISTAN

Music City Bikeway

GALLATIN PIKE

DICKERSON PIKE

FOSTER AVE

NOLENSVILLE PIKE

0   1 mi

0   1 km

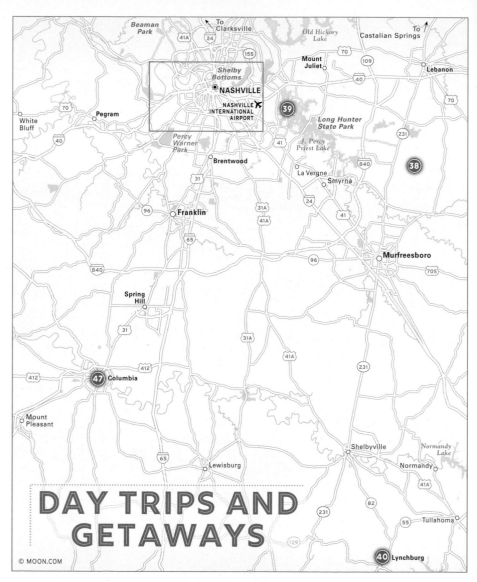

DAY TRIPS AND GETAWAYS

© MOON.COM

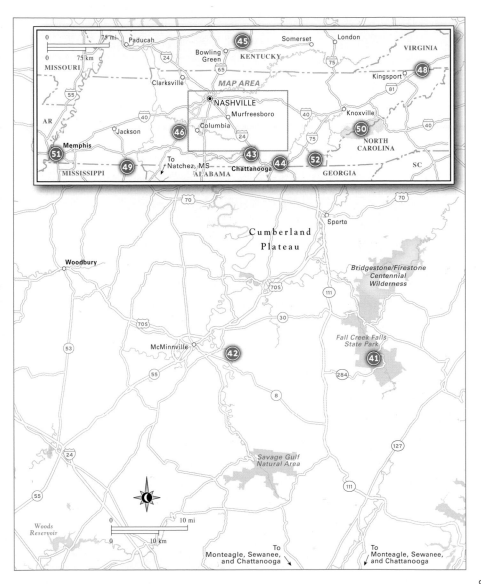

THIS IS MY NASHVILLE

Music City is a transplant's town. We call Nashville natives "unicorns" because so many people who live here came here from somewhere else. They come for the music—to play it, to work in the industry, or just to listen to it—but they also come here because this is a city of people who listen to their own rhythm, people who like to do things differently. That iconoclastic beat is what makes it a fun place to live. There's always something to do that is unusual and creative; and it is often miles away (literally and figuratively) from Lower Broadway's tourist sights and crowds.

When I moved to Nashville more than a decade ago, I started a refrain: "People in Nashville do weird things for a living." And I've spent the years since getting to experience those weird things, be it eating "hot chicken cheese," a gooey vegetarian alternative to the city's iconic dish created by a local chef; or watching a display of entirely indoor fireworks (set to music, of course).

Sometimes Nashville is depicted as a one-note (pun intended) town of beer, bachelorettes, and boots. The real Nashville is more diverse and complex. It boasts the largest Kurdish population in the United States and is home to the National Museum of African American Music. It even owes its nickname, Music City, to one of its historically Black colleges.

We're not just "Music City" or "Nash Vegas." We're "the Athens of the South" and the "buckle of the Bible Belt." Explore all of the nuances of Nashville with these experiences, one for each week of the year. But, yes, of course, you can still wear your cowboy boots.

Corner Music in East Nashville

TO DO LISTS

Live Music

1. Try your hand at **songwriting**
3. Hear sweet music on **Jubilee Day**
7. Kick up your heels at a **honky-tonk**
14. Learn to **two-step** or **line dance**
17. Hear **up-and-coming musicians** first
18. Celebrate Latin America at **Plaza Mariachi**
24. Strum and pick your way through **local guitar shops**

Food

2 Savor Southern cuisine at a **meat-and-three**

9 Take a fork to some tender **barbecue**

11 Snack, shop, and swim on **Dickerson Pike**

18 Celebrate Latin America at **Plaza Mariachi**

21 Play with your food at **family-friendly restaurants**

25 Feed your mind in **North Nashville**

27 Feast on **Kurdish food**

31 Make your eyes water sampling **hot chicken**

33 Lunch at an **old-timer restaurant**

36 Taste the international flavors of **Nolensville Pike**

38 Taste Tennessee's bounty at **U-Pick-Em farms**

Black Heritage

- ③ Hear sweet music on **Jubilee Day**
- ⑥ Celebrate Black culture and history on **Jefferson Street**
- ⑬ Relive the **Nashville sit-ins**
- ㉕ Feed your mind in **North Nashville**
- ㊱ Follow in the footsteps of Civil Rights activists in **Memphis**

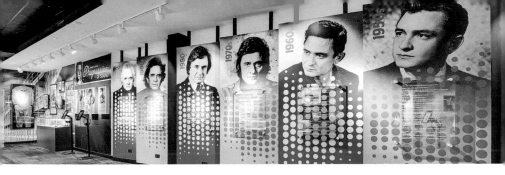

Art and Culture

⑮ Create a masterpiece at a **makerspace**

⑯ Get collegiate in the **Athens of the South**

㉖ Rhapsodize about your favorites at **music museums**

㉜ Get hands-on at **kid-friendly museums**

㉟ Wander the **Buchanan Arts District**

㊼ Meet makers and mules in **Columbia**

㊽ Trace the origins of country music to **Bristol**

Only in Nashville

❶ Try your hand at **songwriting**

❷ Savor Southern cuisine at a **meat-and-three**

❼ Kick up your heels at a **honky-tonk**

⓬ Go backstage at the **Ryman Auditorium**

⓭ Relive the **Nashville sit-ins**

⓮ Learn to **two-step** or **line dance**

⓰ Get collegiate in the **Athens of the South**

㉖ Rhapsodize about your favorites at **music museums**

㉘ Treat yourself to **custom-made boots**

㉚ Get deep into country music at the **Hall of Fame**

㉛ Make your eyes water sampling **hot chicken**

Be a Tourist in Your City

- ⑦ Kick up your heels at a **honky-tonk**
- ⑩ Widen your perspective at historic **Fort Negley**
- ⑫ Go backstage at the **Ryman Auditorium**
- ⑳ Embrace the kitsch at **Madame Tussauds Wax Museum**
- ㉒ Get the best views of the city from the **John Seigenthaler Pedestrian Bridge**
- ㉓ Toast the legacy of **Printers Alley**
- ㉚ Get deep into country music at the **Hall of Fame**
- ㉜ Get hands-on at **kid-friendly museums**

Shopping

④ Shop local in **East Nashville**

⑧ Scope out vintage gems on **Gallatin Pike**

⑪ Snack, shop, and swim on **Dickerson Pike**

⑲ Shop and sip in **The Nations**

㉔ Strum and pick your way through **local guitar shops**

㉘ Treat yourself to **custom-made boots**

㉞ Go to **Nashville Fashion Week** in style

㉟ Wander the **Buchanan Arts District**

Families and Kids

⑤ Pedal the **Music City Bikeway**

⑱ Celebrate Latin America at **Plaza Mariachi**

⑳ Embrace the kitsch at **Madame Tussauds Wax Museum**

㉑ Play with your food at **family-friendly restaurants**

㉜ Get hands-on at **kid-friendly museums**

㊲ Lace up your boots for an **urban hike**

㊳ Taste Tennessee's bounty at **U-Pick-Em farms**

㊸ Escape to **Monteagle and Sewanee**

㊺ Go underground at **Mammoth Cave**

Neighborhoods and City Streets

Outdoor Adventures

5 Pedal the **Music City Bikeway**

10 Widen your perspective at historic **Fort Negley**

37 Lace up your boots for an **urban hike**

39 **Kayak** and **paddleboard** on Percy Priest Lake

41 Go chasing **waterfalls**

42 Dig deep in a **Tennessee cave**

44 Climb, bike, and paddle in **Chattanooga**

45 Go underground at **Mammoth Cave**

50 Witness the mountain magic of the **Smokies**

52 Get soaked **whitewater rafting** on the Ocoee River

Day Trips

- **39** **Kayak** and **paddleboard** on Percy Priest Lake
- **40** Sip your way down the **Tennessee Whiskey Trail**
- **41** Go chasing **waterfalls**
- **42** Dig deep in a **Tennessee cave**
- **45** Go underground at **Mammoth Cave**
- **46** Drive the **Natchez Trace Parkway**
- **47** Meet makers and mules in **Columbia**

The Bristol Sessions and Circles of Success
From Location Recordings to Lasting Legacies

Weekend Getaways

1 Try your hand at songwriting

Live Music • Only in Nashville

Why Go: Take a class to learn how songwriters develop their craft. And who knows? Maybe you'll get a writing contract out of it.

Where: Songwriting classes and performances happen all over town.

Timing: Most listening rooms host performances in the early evening, occasionally with a second later at night. Weekend songwriter brunches are becoming popular. The annual **Tin Pan South Songwriters Festival** is where you can really see what goes into blending melody and lyrics.

Telling stories in song is at the core of country music, and Nashville has turned it into an art form. Countless people come to Nashville to turn their stories into music. If you're among that group, or just want to know what goes into crafting a good song, you can take a songwriting class or attend a performance at a listening room.

The Listening Room Cafe

Many songwriters offer one-on-one instruction on how to put a song together. Come prepared with ideas about what you want to write; your instructor will help you move the "plot" of your story forward. Here are some options to help you find a class.

From its headquarters on Music Row, the **Nashville Songwriters Association International** (1710 Roy Acuff Pl., 615/236-3354, www.nashvillesongwriters.com) offers weekly songwriting workshops. You'll need to pay to join NSAI, which will give you unlimited access to their workshops. You can also book sessions in writing rooms that have all the gear you need to collaborate with others. The **Tennessee Songwriters Association International** (2416 Music Valley Dr., 615/582-0176, www.tennsongwriters.com) near Opryland has similar offerings for its members.

From its shop in East Nashville, **Fanny's House of Music** (1101 Holly St., 615/750-5746, www.fannyshouseofmusic.com) has offered classes taught by local songwriters and musicians

The Bluebird Café

The Listening Room Cafe

for years. In 2020, the owners started a nonprofit organization called Fanny's School of Music. Both the shop and the school focus on opportunities for female and nonbinary students and teachers. Fanny's offers one-on-one classes as well as the chance to build your own group class with a few friends.

The best way to learn songwriting is to do it, of course. But the second-best way is to head to a listening room and hear for yourself what other songwriters are doing. A listening room is a place where songwriters perform acoustically and share the stories behind their lyrics. In some cases, they'll tell you how they sold the song that became a hit—and it will sound different from the writer's mouth than it does on the radio. Many listening rooms are set up "in the round," meaning several songwriters will be on stage together and take turns playing a tune and bantering with one another. Listening rooms are quiet spots; please don't talk during performances. You also won't find any fancy stage design: The emphasis is on the singer and the song. Here are some of the best listening rooms in the city:

The Bluebird Café (4104 Hillsboro Pike, 615/383-1461, http://bluebirdcafe.com) is Nashville's most famous listening room. The Bluebird is famous for its songwriters' nights, open mics, and performances in the round. Musicians aren't up on a stage—they are on the floor with you. Since it's a small room, reservations are required—and they are tough to come by. Get on the website in the morning a few weeks before you want to see a show and be ready to nab your ticket. The Bluebird is all ages, except for its 10 bar seats, which are only for patrons 21 and older. Note: You will be shushed if you talk here.

The Listening Room Cafe (618 4th Ave. S., 615/259-3600, http://listeningroomcafe. com) in SoBro has become a destination for both locals and tourists. The space here is bigger than some other listening rooms, with large communal tables, but it's still small enough that you can hear the writers' stories and witness them rib and praise each other onstage. The food here, particularly the biscuits, is a draw all on its own.

Commodore Grille (2613 West End Ave., 615/327-4707) is nestled in the lobby of the Holiday Inn near the Vanderbilt campus. While its location may seem odd, it has become a favorite listening room for Nashville singer-songwriters who want to perform in a quiet place with a positive vibe. You can call ahead to get the lineup of performers, but it's a reliable ro-

Local Lore

Songwriting is all about collaboration. The "Nashville co-write" is an industry method that pairs songwriters together to craft a song. Since the 1980s, music publishers have been deliberately matching writers with different strengths, setting them up in a room with a few guitars (and maybe a few beers), and hoping they emerge with some hit songs. Look at the credits from any of your favorite tunes; you'll likely see more than one name listed as the writer...and you have Nashville to thank for that.

tation of talented locals, so you can just as easily show up and be impressed. The happy hour specials are a nice incentive to get there early.

Bobby's Idle Hour (9 Music Square S., 615/649-8530, www.bobbysidlehour.com) has been at different locations around Music Row over the decades. All the while, it has remained a dependable, low-key place to have a cheap beer and hear songwriters share their stories. The small stage has just enough room for a few guitarists and microphones.

Connect with...

⑫ Go backstage at the Ryman Auditorium

⑰ Hear up-and-coming musicians first

㉔ Strum and pick your way through local guitar shops

2 Savor Southern cuisine at a meat-and-three

Food • Only in Nashville

Why Go: The meat-and-three cafeteria is a Nashville institution, where you can eat food like Mama made—even if your mama didn't cook like this.

Where: Citywide, but concentrated around Germantown, Midtown, and The Gulch. The best way to identify a meat-and-three is to look for a line out the door at midday.

Timing: Meat-and-threes serve comfort food. Go when the weather starts to cool off in fall and you want something warm and comforting. Many of these spots are open for lunch only, so go at lunchtime on a day when you can take a nap afterward.

There's a hilarious scene in the first season of the Netflix show *Master of None* where Aziz Ansari's character, Dev, takes a woman on a whirlwind date from New York to Nashville. They're standing in line ordering dinner, but Rachel, Dev's date, can't find any vegetarian-friendly options. The restaurant manager assures Rachel he can build her something to eat from sides. He brings her a tray with a meager offering: a square of cornbread, a cup of pickles, and a banana. The scene is funny because it's true. (I admit: I saved a screenshot of those sad pickles to look at when I need a laugh.)

Nashville has long been known for its lack of vegetarian food (though it is becoming more common). Contributing to that legacy is the meat-and-three, a cafeteria-style restaurant that serves one meat dish and three vegetables on the side. (Sometimes the restaurant serves an entrée and two sides; this is still called a meat-and-three.) Such eateries are dotted all over the South, but have a particular concentration in Nashville, where they have become their own category of local cuisine, second only to hot chicken.

A meat-and-three is the great equalizer. There's nothing fancy: The decor will be low-key, and you'll carry your own tray. A meat-and-three is where you will see folks from every segment of Nashville life—politicians, academics, tourists, construction workers, and celebrities—stand in the same line. No one, not even the celebrities, can reserve a table in advance during a lunch rush. You have to go through the line, pay, and then wait for an open table, no matter how

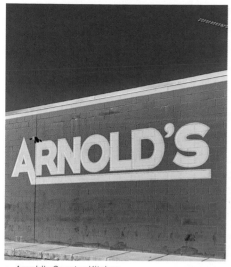

 Arnold's Country Kitchen

▲ Swett's Restaurant

▲ Swett's Restaurant

many gold records you have. (And no matter how many gold records you have, you may end up with squash casserole on your sleeve.)

Most meat-and-threes are predictable, but also change their menus regularly. For example, fried chicken may only be available on Fridays; meatloaf only on Thursdays. Once a meat-and-three is sold out, that's probably it for the day. Don't expect anyone to make more creamed corn just because the person in front of you took the last in the pan. Oh, and at a classic meat-and-three, mac and cheese counts as a vegetable...even if it has bacon in it. No matter what's on the menu, the options will be delicious and filling—and probably not cardiologist approved.

Arnold's Country Kitchen (605 8th Ave. S., 615/256-4455, www.arnoldscountrykitchen.com) is the gold-standard. Chef Kahili Arnold has taken the helm at the restaurant his parents started, and he brings a creative sensibility to the classics (there's even a James Beard award in the restaurant's past). Celebrity chef Sean Brock has said that Arnold's is the first place he takes out-of-towners. There are several dozen other time-honored meat-and-threes throughout the city. Among the best is **Swett's Restaurant** (2725 Clifton Ave., 615/329-4418,

▲ Swett's delivery van

Local Lore

In her 2015 cookbook *Nashville Eats,* author Jennifer Justus quoted music journalist Chet Flippo as saying country music record contracts used to come with gravy stains on them, since most deals were signed at a meat-and-three. Contracts nowadays are digital, but you'll still see business lunches taking place at these beloved restaurants.

www.swettsrestaurant.com) in Midtown, which has great beef tips and a good amount of elbow room at its tables. Sophia Vaughn's family has been serving soul food to locals for almost 70 years near Germantown at **Silver Sands Café** (937 Locklayer St., 615/780-9900, www.silversandsnashville.com). In addition to Southern classics, Silver Sands also has tilapia and salmon croquette on the menu.

Like on *Master of None,* at many meat-and-threes, the vegetarian option is to load up on sides. Hopefully, you'll get more than a banana and pickles, but it is worth asking how vegetables are prepared, as many greens are cooked in bacon fat. **JamaicaWay Restaurant** in the Farmers Market (900 Rosa L. Parks Blvd., 615/255-5920, http://jamaicawayrestaurant.com) makes all its dishes without pork. Berry Hill's **Sunflower Café** (2834 Azalea Pl., 615/457-2568, www.sunflowercafenashville.com) is an entirely vegetarian restaurant with many nods to traditional meat-and-three dishes.

Connect with...

25 Feed your mind in North Nashville

Hear sweet music on Jubilee Day

Fisk University

Live Music • Black Heritage

Why Go: This annual event is the first opportunity of the year to hear the melodic voices of the Fisk Jubilee Singers at a poignant performance honoring the choir's storied history.

Where: Fisk University, 1000 17th Ave. N., www.fisk.edu • free to attend

Timing: October 6, rain or shine, is Jubilee Day. Plan to spend a couple of hours at the various events and walking through the Fisk University campus.

The choir performs concerts around the city, including at the Ryman Auditorium, for the length of the academic year, so there are other opportunities to hear them sing if you miss out on Jubilee Day.

Jubilee Day is my favorite day of the year in Nashville, a day when I feel connected to those who were here before me, and a day when I feel hopeful for the connections we will make going forward.

First, some history. In 1871, Fisk University was struggling. The historically Black college was using old Union army barracks to house students. The school was just five years old, but its infrastructure was already decaying while more Black students were seeking the higher education Fisk provided. The school needed some cash. So, in what might now be considered a very Nashville idea, the nine-person school choir withdrew all the money from the university's treasury and set out on a world tour. (In the U.S., their route followed the Underground Railroad, and many of these concerts were secret affairs.) Remembering a biblical reference to the "year of the jubilee," Fisk treasurer and choir manager George White gave the choir their name—the Fisk Jubilee Singers. By 1874, they were successful enough that the school was able to build its first permanent building, the aptly named **Jubilee Hall.**

Every October 6, the school hosts Jubilee Day to honor the day in 1871 when the choir departed Fisk to see the world and secure the school's future. The day kicks off with a convocation in the school's Victorian-style **Memorial Chapel,** featuring the current Jubilee Singers. Each

Fisk Jubilee Singers

Cravath Hall, Fisk University

Jubilee Hall

year, new students audition and join the choir. (Today's choir is mixed-gender and larger than the original nine.) This performance is their first of the academic year; the singers perform time-honored spirituals and gospel music. The convocation's service recalls the struggles and the triumph of the original choir. Featured speakers, ranging from Fisk alumni to Civil Rights leaders, draw parallels to modern times.

Before the day's events begin, current Fisk students gather leaves from the magnolia trees on campus and make wreaths to place on the graves of four of the original Jubilee Singers who are buried in town. After the convocation, a caravan drives through town to two different cemeteries to lay these wreaths and pay respects. Other campus-based events take place throughout the day, including free access to the remarkable **Carl Van Vechten Gallery** (www.fisk.edu/galleries), which houses part of a collection once owned by Alfred Stieglitz. It is also worth stopping at the smaller **Aaron Douglas Gallery,** which houses Fisk's collection of African, African American, and folk art works. At night, there's typically a concert on campus that helps

Memorial Chapel

Local Lore

The Fisk Jubilee Singers set out across the ocean in 1871, where the United Kingdom's Queen Victoria was so amazed by their voices that she is said to have exclaimed, "You must come from some kind of music city." And, well, you already know that the nickname stuck.

raise money for the current singers' annual scholarship fund and to keep the choir singing all year.

I love gazing at the university's architecture and inhaling the scent of the magnolias as I walk across campus. I head over to **Cravath Hall** and look at the powerful **Aaron Douglas murals** that are tucked away in rooms on the second floor. Douglas was a painter and illustrator during the Harlem Renaissance who established Fisk's first formal art department, and is known as the father of African American art. These murals depict Black figures in classic art settings, fusing Greek and Roman symbols with African American figures. The murals are one of the city's unsung gems, just like Jubilee Day.

Connect with...

6 Celebrate Black culture and history on Jefferson Street
16 Get collegiate in the Athens of the South
25 Feed your mind in North Nashville

4 Shop local in East Nashville

Neighborhoods and City Streets • Shopping

Why Go: Nashville's very essence—scrappy, creative, joyful, perplexing—plays out in the city's east side, thanks to a collection of small businesses and the people who run them.

Where: The majority of the exploration here is in walking distance of the Five Points area, where 10th Street, Main Street, and Woodland Street meet.

Timing: Head over in the early afternoon to stroll the shops and stay through the evening to have a cocktail and dinner as the sun sets.

Just east of downtown, on the other side of the Cumberland River, begins East Nashville, a collection of smaller neighborhoods—Lockeland Springs, Dickerson Pike, Cleveland Park, and Five Points—known for their eclectic sensibilities, food scenes, and musician residents. East Nashville prides itself on being eccentric: This is a part of town with undeniably quirky stores, such as **The Donut Distillery** (311 Gallatin Ave., 615/678-8685, https://donutdistillery.com), which makes bourbon-infused doughnuts. You won't find any big box stores here. Some residents, myself included, occasionally challenge themselves to do all their errands without crossing the river to get to "the mainland."

East Nashville is a neighborhood that honors its past. It's where "The Devil Went Down to Georgia" was recorded. It's home to the bar where Johnny Cash spent his 70th birthday. **Lockeland Table** (1520 Woodland St., 615/228-4864, www.lockelandtable.com), one of the city's best restaurants, designed its exterior to look like the original 1930s dry goods store that once stood in its place. (Inside, check out the photos of the building through the ages.) But East Nashville is also an area that looks to the future, supporting the small businesses that seem to crop up every day.

As the area's popularity has increased, so have its real estate prices, making it harder for small businesses to survive. **The Shoppes on Fatherland** (1006 Fatherland St., 615/227-8646, http://fatherlanddistrict.com) is one response to this dilemma. More than 20 tiny busi-

1: Bongo Java **2:** The Shoppes on Fatherland
3: Five Points Alley Shops **4:** Hunters Station

▲ Lockeland Table

nesses are housed in equally small storefronts here, selling handmade goods and repurposed vintage items. Some of the stores have very specific niches: If you need a custom-made Western wear onesie for your baby or a themed dog collar, you'll find it here. The complex offers a strong community vibe and a fun energy. Some business owners use their storefronts to test the retail waters before they move to bigger spaces. Some businesses pop up just for the holiday season, while others are stalwarts that have been here for years.

The **Five Points Alley Shops** (1108 Woodland St., 615/226-2070, http://c615.co) is another collection of quirky, brightly colored storefronts, and it's within walking distance of The Shoppes on Fatherland. It's home to more than 10 micro-businesses, including a used bookstore, a home goods shop, a vintage clothing store, an art gallery, a letterpress stationery shop, and a store selling vintage cowboy boots. Outside the shops you'll find lovely, small gardens.

Hunters Station (975 Main St., www.huntersstation.com) is the dining equivalent of The Shoppes on Fatherland and Five Points Alley Shops. A food hall that opened in an old automotive supply shop, Hunters Station is home to as many as 10 local restaurants, all orga-

Community Focus

While today it is a small business hub, East Nashville went through a lot to get to this point. The neighborhood has borne the brunt of both natural and political disasters. Tornadoes ravaged this area in 1933, 1998, and again in March 2020. There's also the 1916 fire, the 1927 flood, and the post-World War II governmental policies that caused some historic homes to be demolished to make way for newer housing.

In many ways, it was the 1998 tornado that transformed East Nashville into what it is today. That was the same year the NFL's Tennessee Titans (then the Tennessee Oilers) came to town. Nissan Stadium opened in the neighborhood in 1999, giving people a reason to visit the city's east side. Soon after that, the prominent local coffee chain **Bongo Java** (107 S. 11th St., 615/777-3278, www.bongojava.com/bongo-east) moved to East Nashville, helping to further revitalize the neighborhood. (Today, this location shares space with a board game café.)

nized around communal seating areas (both indoor and outdoor). The complex also houses a community kitchen that small food businesses can use without having to lease their own space. Try their bagels, smoothies, and sweet treats for yourself at **Citizen Market,** one of Hunters Station's tenants. The other restaurants at Hunters Station sell goodies like grilled cheese sandwiches, burgers, milkshakes, and tacos.

Thanks to these retail spaces that encourage small businesses and allow them to thrive, East Nashville has grown into a community of entrepreneurs—people who are willing to try new things, even ones that seem silly or unsustainable. This neighborhood is understandably proud of its restaurants, bars, shops, and music venues. If you haven't yet visited from the mainland, give it a try. I have no doubt you'll find something to your taste.

Connect with...

8 Scope out vintage gems on Gallatin Pike
11 Snack, shop, and swim on Dickerson Pike

5 Pedal the Music City Bikeway

Outdoor Adventures • Families and Kids

Why Go: With enough pedal power you can explore the entirety of Nashville via the Music City Bikeway. And you don't even need to have your own bike.

Where: The bikeway runs 26 miles across the city, spanning from Percy Priest Lake to Percy Warner Park • http://maps.nashville.gov/MusicCityBikeway

Timing: Pick a day when the weather is cooperating. Fall tends to offer perfect temperatures and less rain.

Nashville doesn't have the cycling cred of some other cities. It's certainly not Copenhagen, with its claim of more bikes than people. But exploring Nashville by bike is becoming increasingly popular and easy to do, thanks to bike lanes, multimodal streets, and rental bike stations all over town. There's a bike route for every kind of cyclist here.

There are more than 90 miles of greenways and 133 miles of on-road bike lanes and shared-use bike routes in the city. Primary among them is the 26-mile-long Music City Bikeway. Developed as a way of connecting many of the city's greenways, the bikeway covers a variety of terrain, from bucolic forested parks to busy downtown streets. It winds its way across the entire city, stretching from the Percy Priest Dam at I-40 in the east to Percy Warner Park in the west. Eight miles of the bikeway include streets with designated bike lanes, some of which are just a painted lane, while others have barriers between the bike lane and vehicular traffic.

The bikeway goes right by the Nashville Farmers' Market, so you can park your ride at one of the creatively shaped bike racks (think giant sliced tomatoes and oversized cornstalks) and browse the produce and craft stands. All along the bikeway, you'll encounter lots of public art. On the **Shelby Bottoms Greenway,** pause to snap a photo of *Reflection,* a giant mockingbird sculpted from stainless steel. You'll ride through neighborhoods that are ripe with places to stop for a drink or meal, and past views of the Cumberland River. You'll also weave through industrial parks and ride alongside traffic in some areas.

▲ Music City Bikeway

▲ B-Cycle

The city's detailed bike maps (available online) include mileages, directions on where to turn, and different access points on the bikeway. The city also publishes a map called "The Groove," which highlights interlocking bike routes within five miles of downtown. If you aren't excited about tackling one of Nashville's many hills or zooming between cars, rest assured that some parts of the bikeway are flatter and have less traffic. **Walk Bike Nashville** (www.walkbikenashville.org/maps) offers maps of biking routes that avoid steep hills and follow car-free pathways when possible. These routes are especially good for kids. Keep an eye out for **Open Streets Nashville** (www.openstreetsnashville.org) in September, an annual event that closes some neighborhood streets to cars, making them more pedestrian- and cyclist-friendly.

If you need a good bike shop to get you on your way, there's at least one in every part of town. Some options include **Shelby Avenue Bicycle Co.** (1629 Shelby Ave., 615/924-3274, www.greenfleetbikes.com) in East Nashville, **Green Fleet Bicycle Shop** (934 Jefferson St., 615/379-8687, www.greenfleetbikes.com) in Germantown, **Cumberland Transit** (2807 West End Ave., 615/321-4069, http://cumberlandtransit.com) near the Vanderbilt campus, and

Trace Bikes (8080B Hwy. 100, 615/646-2485, www.tracebikes.com) on the west side, which helps folks gear up to cycle the Natchez Trace Parkway.

If you don't have a bike, you can still enjoy the city on two wheels. With a local ID, city residents can check out a bike from **Nashville GreenBikes** (www.nashville.gov) for free from one of a number of Metro Park community centers. **B-Cycle** (http://nashville.bcycle.com) rents bikes out for 24 hours for just $5 plus an hourly rental fee (frequent users can get a membership). There are more than 36 B-Cycle stations across town. The bikes come with baskets, but not helmets, so bring your own.

When biking on the greenways, adhere to the 15-mph speed limit. Call out to pedestrians and fellow cyclists when passing ("On your left" works). Bikers must yield to pedestrians. And watch out for young kids and dogs, who might dart unexpectedly across your path.

Connect with...

37 Lace up your boots for an urban hike

6 Celebrate Black culture and history on Jefferson Street

Neighborhoods and City Streets • Black Heritage

Why Go: Jefferson Street is a historically Black neighborhood and an essential part of Nashville, home to a decades-long history that includes the Civil Rights Movement and a legendary music scene.

Where: About 2.5 miles north of downtown, Jefferson Street runs east-west. The locations covered here focus on the area between 12th Ave. N. and 28th Ave. N.

Timing: The Jefferson Street Sound Museum is only open on Saturdays (or by appointment). Daytime is best for exploring this neighborhood on foot, so plan to stroll before or after your museum tour.

Walking down Jefferson Street, you'll witness a busy city thoroughfare, with cars and bikes whizzing by and sidewalks full of people patronizing small businesses. The buildings run the gamut from historic stone-and-brick edifices to new construction. There are empty lots, vacant one-story homes with boarded up windows, and otherwise nondescript structures adorned with vivid murals. In the background are the hum of the nearby interstate and the mouth-watering smells emanating from barbecue smokers in parking lots.

For more than a century, Jefferson Street has been the heart of Black Nashville, a vibrant community with theaters, music clubs, bakeries, and grocery stores. Nearby are three HBCUs: Fisk University, Meharry Medical College, and Tennessee State University. Starting in the 1940s and spanning several decades, Jefferson Street was also home to a blues and R&B scene that's not quite as famous as the city's other musical legacy. Icons like Little Richard, Ray Charles, and Etta James all performed in the clubs on Jefferson Street. Even Jimi Hendrix spent some of his musically formative years living and playing here.

The neighborhood also boasts ties to the Civil Rights Movement. Much of the organizing for Nashville's sit-ins and other protests took place here, led by college students, many from TSU and Fisk; Jefferson Street was where they could conveniently meet to organize. The still-active **Clark Memorial United Methodist Church** (1014 14th Ave. N., www.clarkumcnashville.

Alkebu-Lan Images Bookstore & Gifts

Jefferson Street Sound Museum

org) is where nonviolence training for the protests took place in 1958. A stop on the U.S. Civil Rights Trail, the church also hosted annual meetings for Martin Luther King Jr.'s Southern Christian Leadership Conference.

In 1956, the Interstate Highway Act irrevocably changed Jefferson Street. When I-40 was built, the Black community was literally cut off from the economic engine of the rest of the city. Despite community organizing, lawsuits, and even an appeal to the U.S. Supreme Court, more than 16 blocks of Jefferson Street were bulldozed in 1968. Within a year of I-40 opening, many of Jefferson Street's businesses closed. Residents no longer had essential shops within walking distance. Property values dropped by one-third.

Desegregation made it easier for some families to move away from the historically Black neighborhood. Others, like Lorenzo Washington, stayed to rebuild and preserve its legacy. Washington owns the **Jefferson Street Sound Museum** (2004 Jefferson St., 615/414-6675). He calls it a "mini museum," but that downplays the importance of his considerable knowledge and his collection. He offers hour-long tours of the space, which is stocked with artifacts like guitars, posters, and vinyl records, all a testament to the neighborhood's long musical history, spanning 1940-1970. Washington also runs a recording studio in the same building. It was here in 2013 that Marion James, who is known as Nashville's "Queen of the Blues," recorded the song "Back in the Day." The mural out front depicts some of the legends who performed at the clubs on Jefferson Street.

Many of Jefferson Street's once-famous edifices, like the Ritz theater, are gone, but others remain. Across the street from the Jefferson Street Sound Museum stands **Citizens Bank** (2013 Jefferson St.), believed to be the oldest continually operating minority-owned bank in the country. It's still responsible for loaning to many of the businesses in the area today.

Balance the history tour by patronizing a few of the neighborhood's local businesses. **Alkebu-Lan Images Bookstore & Gifts** (2721 Jefferson St., 615/321-4111) stocks books and t-shirts. **Woodcuts Gallery and Framing** (1613 Jefferson St., 615/321-5357, www.woodcutsfineartgallery.com) specializes in African art. Since 1966, **The College Crib** (2719 Jefferson St., 615/329-3885, www.collegecrib.com) has been emblazoning shirts, jackets, stoles, and other items with Black sorority and fraternity letters. They also sell personalized gear for family reunions. **One Drop Ink Tattoo Parlour and Gallery** (1511 Jefferson St., 615/649-

1106, https://onedropink.com), is a tattoo studio and a fine art gallery. Owner Elisheba Israel Mrozik operates her shop as a gathering place for neighborhood artists, displaying artwork, hosting art crawls, and painting murals on the side of the building.

Of course, you'll need something to eat. For a sit-down meal, opt for jerk chicken and plantain puffs from **Riddim n Spice** (2116 Meharry Blvd., 615/953-7121), one block south of Jefferson Street. **Ooh Wee Bar-B-Q** (2008 Jefferson St., 615/200-7191, http://orderoohweebarbq.com) is known for its $1 turkey legs. Take your food to go and have a picnic at a scenic college campus or park. **Hadley Park** (1037 28th Ave. N.) was one of the first public parks in the country intended solely for African Americans when it was opened in 1912. **Kossie Gardner Sr. Park** (1606 Jefferson St.) is named after the Black entrepreneur who opened the funeral home across the street to serve African American families.

For more information on Jefferson Street's history, watch Nashville Public Television's documentary *Facing North: Jefferson Street* (www.wnpt.org/jefferson-street) or listen to the episode of the *Curious Nashville* podcast (https://wpln.org) called "The Year Jimi Hendrix Jammed on Jefferson Street and How It Still Reverberates."

Connect with...
- ❸ Hear sweet music on Jubilee Day
- ⓭ Relive the Nashville sit-ins
- ㉟ Wander the Buchanan Arts District

Kick up your heels at a honky-tonk

Only in Nashville • Live Music • Be a Tourist in Your City

Why Go: The honky-tonk is what makes Music City sing. These bars are where you can dance with abandon, feeding off the energy of talented musicians.

Where: Broadway is also sometimes called Honky-Tonk Row. There are honky-tonks in other parts of town, but the four blocks of Broadway between 1st Avenue and Rep. John Lewis Way are teeming with them.

Timing: Most honky-tonks open before noon, but you want to go at night. There's a sweet spot in the early evenings during the week when the bands are playing, but the bars aren't overwhelmed, so you can really kick up your feet and dance. Weekends can be heavy on crowds and cover bands playing rock rather than Western swing.

Honky-tonk is a type of live music also called Western swing, an upbeat subset of country that's more similar to jazz than to the sad ballads that you might typically associate with country music. A honky-tonk is also the type of bar where you'll hear that music, and to top it off, it's the name of the dance you'll be doing there. That sounds confusing, but in context it makes sense. When someone says, "Let's go honky-tonking," just know you're about to experience Nashville's roots, its raison d'être—and you're practically guaranteed to have a good time. (And a few cheap beers, if that's your thing. Honky-tonks are fun, but they aren't fancy.)

There are a number of honky-tonks on Broadway, so you can go from one to another until you find a band and a crowd that you groove with. Once you're at a spot you like, whether you're perched on a bar stool or out on the dance floor, plan to stick around for a while. Most honky-tonks are all ages during the day but convert to 21 and up after 6pm. They typically don't have a cover charge. When the cowboy hat is passed for the band, don't forget to drop a few dollars in.

Here are your best bets for listening—and dancing—to Nashville's most iconic sound:

A cozy, dark dance hall, **Layla's** (418 Broadway, 615/726-2799, www.laylasnashville.com) offers a fun honky-tonk trifecta: cheap beer, a hot dog cart, and no cover. It's often standing room only on Friday and Saturday nights, but that's not the only time to hear good music. Al-

Layla's

Robert's Western World

Nudie's Honky Tonk

most any time the lights are on, it's worth stepping inside. Head to the back entrance (which opens onto the alley next to the Ryman) or the upper floor for more space. This is the only woman-owned honky-tonk on Broadway.

Nudie's Honky Tonk (409 Broadway, www.nudieshonkytonk.com) may be one of the newer honky-tonks on Lower Broad (it opened in 2016), but it has a serious connection to the past. This bar celebrates all things Nudie Cohn. Nudie was the tailor who made suits for Johnny Cash and Elvis, among others. The bar is also a museum, with many of Nudie's famous works behind glass and one of his ostentatious cars, a $400,000 Cadillac El Dorado, hanging from the wall. The dance floor is small so it can be crowded here, but the music is loud, and a good time is inevitable.

Robert's Western World (416 Broadway, 615/244-9552, http://robertswesternworld. com) is often voted the city's best honky-tonk by locals. Originally a store selling Western regalia, Robert's morphed into a bar and nightclub with a good gift shop—yes, you can still buy boots here. Many of the city's honky-tonks can start to blend together, but the upbeat energy makes it feel different from the rest. Robert's books some of the city's best musicians—and that's saying something. Hungry? Try the famous Recession Special, a fried bologna sandwich with chips and a PBR for five bucks.

The Stage on Broadway (412 Broadway, 615/726-0504, www.thestageonbroadway. com) is a honky-tonk that often plays second fiddle to Robert's and Layla's, but gets its fair share of movie and TV cameo appearances thanks to an iconic neon sign that features a guitar wearing a cowboy hat. It has a large dance floor and live music seven nights a week.

Country megastar Alan Jackson bought one of Lower Broad's longtime honky-tonks, then called The Wheel, and re-opened it in 2016 as **AJ's Good Time Bar** (421 Broadway, 615/678-4808, www.ajsgoodtimebar.com), naming it after one of his most popular songs. Since then, it's been a reliable place to hear country music, albeit more hits than classic Western swing. Running into Jackson here is not a regular occurrence, but it isn't beyond the realm of possibility.

As Broadway has gotten more popular and rents have gotten higher, some of the best honky-tonk action has moved farther away from downtown:

Nashville Palace (2412 Music Valley Pl., 615/889-1541) near Opryland, is an old-school honky-tonk: nothing fancy, just good music, affordable drinks, and lots of room to dance. The

Palace hires many of the city's long-time musicians and offers pre-concert dance lessons on occasion.

Dee's Country Cocktail Lounge (102 Palestine Ave., 615/852-8827, http://deeslounge. com) is in the suburban neighborhood of Madison, just a few minutes north of East Nashville. The aesthetics are reminiscent of a 1970s hipster hangout, but it still has the vibe of a honky-tonk, thanks to a large dance floor and a schedule of musicians who play Western swing and other classic country music.

A few spots offer dance lessons in the afternoons or early evenings, including **Honky-Tonk Tuesday Nights,** which takes place at the **American Legion 82** (3204 Gallatin Pike, 615/228-3598) with the house band playing in full Western garb. But it isn't essential to know any specific moves to have a good time. Just grab a partner and follow the crowd.

Connect with...

12 Go backstage at the Ryman Auditorium
14 Learn to two-step or line dance
23 Toast the legacy of Printers Alley

Scope out vintage gems on Gallatin Pike

Shopping • Neighborhoods and City Streets

Why Go: Every musician with stage presence has a signature item, be it a rhinestone jacket, a pair of boots, or a guitar strap. Seek out your own piece at the city's best vintage shops.

Where: While there are vintage shops all over town, Inglewood and East Nashville have a concentration of must-browse options. The ones mentioned here go from north to south on Gallatin Pike, starting at the intersection with Briley Parkway.

Timing: Stores may be picked over before a major event in town, so go early if you're looking for something to wear during Tin Pan South, CMA Music Fest, or the Americana Music Festival. Halloween and New Year's Eve are high-demand events, too.

Because vintage goods are one-of-a-kind, no store has the same stuff—or even the same vibe. Here's a look at some of the city's best.

For vintage clothing with an unapologetic sensibility, head to the two-story **High Class Hillbilly** (4604 Gallatin Pike, 615/840-7328, http://highclasshillbilly.com). Owner Nikki Lane stocks the shop with vintage goods, like leather, denim, and turquoise jewelry, as well as some upcycled pieces, like painted jackets, and custom-made merch, including patches and t-shirts. She has a specific aesthetic, and it is reflected in her cozy, curated shop. Lane is a master at finding surprising treasures, like that box of classic concert t-shirts that's been sitting in someone's basement.

Right next door to High Class Hillbilly is **Backslide Vintage** (4606 Gallatin Pike, 615/649-8562), owned by Zack Smith and Caitlin Doyle-Smith, the voices of Americana duo Smooth Hound Smith. The racks are jam-packed with men's and women's apparel, so you'll need to do some digging and sorting. You'll snag a lot of '70s-style clothes and accessories, and even instruments and furniture in a space that is part thrift store, part living room, and part backstage dressing room. The shop is brightly lit, with high ceilings and big windows.

In a large warehouse-like space with a glittering gold floor, **Old Made Good** (3701B

Old Made Good

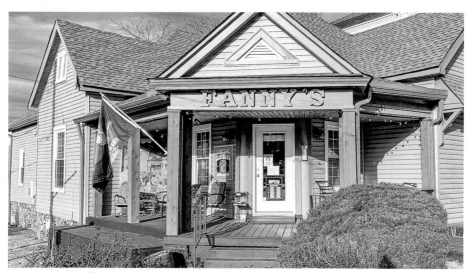

Fanny's House of Music and Pink Star Vintage

Gallatin Pike, 615/432-2882, http://oldmadegoodnashville.bigcartel.com) is chock-full of secondhand items, many of which have been upcycled to give them a unique twist. Search for mid-century modern furniture, original art, turquoise jewelry, and period clothing here. Owner Ashley Sheehan makes art from paintings and textiles she finds, and more often than not the pieces include profanities.

Even if you don't care about vintage clothes, you might want to check out the restored firehouse that is home to **Black Shag Vintage** (1220 Gallatin Ave., 615/626-1606, http://black-shagvintage.com). From the outside, the brick-and-stone building is a head-turner; it stands out from the surrounding new construction. Once inside, you'll be treated to organized racks of biker-chic clothing. Owner Tommy Daley is a former music industry exec who knows what rock stars should wear and can help you find the right outfit for your look.

Star Struck Vintage Nashville (604 Gallatin Pike, 615/679-9675, www.starstruck-vintage.com) is a New York transplant. This vintage store is in a funky strip mall that belies its large interior. Inside you will find 3,000 square feet of merchandise packed onto shelves and racks. The focus here is on clothing from the 1920s to the 1980s, including velvet dresses, fringed jackets, concert t-shirts, lettermen jackets, and other pieces that will look good on stage. Be prepared to spend some time going through all the inventory.

Two blocks west of Star Struck, **Relik Vintage** (730 McFerrin Ave., 615/689-1845, www.relikvintage.com/home) is for those with a more casual vibe. T-shirts, sports jerseys, and dead-stock (old clothing that's never been sold but is in brand-new condition) are on the racks here. The utilitarian space has some plants, artwork, and a mounted deer head, but the t-shirts are the focus.

A beloved East Nashville gem, **Hip Zipper** (1008 Forrest Ave., 615/228-1942, www.hipzipper.com) has been dressing locals in vintage goods since 1999. The focus here is on clothing, which is well organized by size and color. This isn't the kind of place where you ransack bins. Instead, you'll try on the 1970s dress you didn't know you always wanted.

One of the small retailers in the Five Points Alley Shops, **Goodbuy Girls** (1108 Woodland St., 615/281-9447, www.goodbuygirlsnashville.com) is known for its selection of vintage cowboy boots—and the fact that Lady Gaga shopped here once when she was in town. New accessories are mixed in with the vintage wares.

If clothes aren't your thing, head to **Rusty Rats Antique and Vintage** (1006 Fatherland St., 615/797-8834), where the objects of your youth—toys, trophies, lunchboxes, and more—have been turned into art, jewelry, lamps, and great gifts. Rusty Rats is one of the long-time businesses in The Shoppes on Fatherland.

Fanny's House of Music (1101 Holly St., 615/750-5746, www.fannyshouseofmusic.com) is known for its instruments, but the store also shares space with **Pink Star Vintage,** which stocks a selection of well-cared-for men's and women's clothing, jewelry, scarves, hats, and boots. The space is small but well-stocked. While you browse, you'll hear folks testing out Fanny's instruments.

Connect with...

4 Shop local in East Nashville
28 Treat yourself to custom-made boots
34 Go to Nashville Fashion Week in style

9 Take a fork to some tender barbecue

Food

Why Go: This the South. Did you really even eat if you didn't have barbecue?

Where: You can find barbecue almost anywhere you go. Most of the places listed here are concentrated near downtown and East Nashville.

Timing: Late lunch is prime barbecue time. I prefer going in between the lunch and dinner crowds, and late enough in the day that I can be in a food coma after my meal—and not be worried about slogging through work or errands with brisket in my belly.

When people ask me about Nashville barbecue I'm inclined to say, "You're thinking of Memphis." Memphis, Tennessee, and Austin, Texas, have their own barbecue traditions and legacy: Memphis reportedly has more than 100 barbecue joints and is known for pork cooked in a pit. Austin is a brisket town, with the beef cooked low and slow over an oak wood fire. But sometimes you have to give the people what they want. And in recent years, Nashville chefs have done just that, creating a local BBQ culture riffing on all of the tastes of the South.

If smoked meats are your thing, here are some places to dig in. Wherever you go, the meat will have been cooked slow; you shouldn't need to use a knife. You'll get an option of sauces, from vinegar to spicy to sweet. Some places also offer white sauce, a worthy competitor from Northern Alabama.

While **Swett's** (2725 Clifton Ave., 615/329-4418, www.swettsrestaurant.com) is best known as a meat-and-three restaurant, in 2012 the family-owned institution added barbecue to their offerings. That means you can smell the smoker from blocks away and you can get those meat-and-three sides, like real mashed potatoes, vinegary greens, and yeast rolls with your 'cue. In addition to this spot near Tennessee State University, Swett's also has a location in Concourse C at Nashville International Airport and cooks the food at **Johnny Cash's Kitchen & Saloon** (131 3rd Ave. S., 615/209-9504, www.cashkitchenandsaloon.com), which naturally includes barbecue.

1: wings from B&C Market BBQ **2:** pork butt at Edley's Bar-B-Que **3:** Martin's Bar-B-Que Joint **4:** inside Edley's Bar-B-Que

Carey Bringle, the man behind **Peg Leg Porker** (903 Gleaves St., 615/829-6023, https://peglegporker.com) wrote the book on barbecue. Literally: He's the author of *BBQ for Dummies*. You'll find it all at this eatery near the Gulch: barbecue nachos, Kool-Aid pickles (yes, pickles brined in Kool-Aid and, yes, they are delicious), ribs, chicken, pulled pork, beans, and even banana pudding to end your meal.

You'll probably pass **The Gambling Stick** (501 Gallatin Ave., 615/521-9742, www.the-gamblingstick.com) the first time you look for it. I did, and I live in the neighborhood. But you won't miss it again once you try these meats, which are ethically sourced and smoked in small batches. The smoker is in the parking lot and the dining area is a tent. Not that there's anything wrong with that, but if that's not your thing, you can get the goods to go.

The success of **Edley's Bar-B-Que** (908 Main St., 615/873-4085, www.edleysbbq.com) is one of the things that changed people's perception of Nashville as a town with legit barbecue. Since opening in 2011, they've become an essential smoker on the scene, in part because they offer something for every taste, be it pork or brisket or vegetarian options and pork-free sides. In addition to this East Nashville outpost, they also have locations in 12South (2706 12th Ave. S.) and West Nashville (4500 Murphy Rd.).

Walking distance from downtown's honky-tonks and with a great backyard beer garden, **Martin's Bar-B-Que Joint** (410 4th Ave. S., 615/288-0880, www.martinsbbqjoint.com) is one of the city's favorite barbecue houses. It serves pulled pork, barbecue spareribs, smoked wings, and beef brisket, plus all the side dishes you could want: coleslaw, green beans, potato salad, and corn cakes. Martin's has several other locations around town.

B&C Market BBQ (900 Rosa L. Parks Blvd., 615/770-0032, www.baconandcaviar.com) has been in the Nashville Farmers Market since 2008, serving some of the best brisket and vinegar sauce in town. In 2020, two long-time employees bought the joint and are continuing to offer hickory-smoked goodness. Get it to go or eat in the Market House, the open food court inside of the farmers market.

When was the last time you were handed your food through a hole cut in the wall? That's the case at **Mary's Old Fashioned Pit Bar-B-Que** (1106 Jefferson St., 615/256-7696, www.marysbbqpit.com), a Memphis-style barbecue place that is long on flavor, but short on atmo-

Edley's Bar-B-Que in West Nashville

sphere. The standalone restaurant on historic Jefferson Street does have a few tables where you can sit, but all the action is outside, as folks line up at the pickup window.

Shotgun Willie's BBQ (4000 Gallatin Pike, 615/942-9188, http://sgwbbq.com) goes all-in on Texas-style barbecue. You'll find ribs, brisket, chicken, and sausage, plus Texas sheet cake and sides. There's a small patio for dining at this spot in Inglewood, which is north of East Nashville.

Connect with...

㉑ Play with your food at family-friendly restaurants

㉛ Make your eyes water sampling hot chicken

10 Widen your perspective at historic Fort Negley

Outdoor Adventures • Be a Tourist in Your City

Why Go: There are plenty of trendy spots to catch a Nashville view (looking at you, rooftop bars), but Fort Negley combines scenic overlooks with the great outdoors, important history, and an unbeatable (free) price tag.

Where: 1.5 miles south of downtown • 1100 Fort Negley Blvd., 615/862-8470, http://nashville.gov • park: dawn-dusk daily; visitors center (includes museum): noon-4pm Tues.-Thurs., 9am-4pm Fri.-Sat. June-Aug., noon-4pm Tues.-Fri., 9am-4pm Sat. Sept.-May • free admission

Timing: Fort Negley is a year-round draw. Head over in spring when wildflowers dot the hillside, providing a colorful contrast to the cityscape. If you go in summer, you can take advantage of the long days to spend more time absorbing the views.

When I first moved to Nashville, Fort Negley wasn't on my list of must-visit places. Though it was built early in the Civil War, the fort was never challenged in battle, so I figured if I wanted to do a deeper dive into the area's connection to the Civil War, I could hop over to battle sites like **Corinth, Mississippi.** But when I did eventually visit the fort, I was surprised to find that it provided me with new insights into Nashville's past—and glorious views of the city's present.

Early in the Civil War, the Union Army determined that taking and holding Nashville was a critical strategic link in their victory. So, after Nashville fell in 1862, Union forces needed to fortify the city against attacks—and quickly. Fort Negley was built in just five months in late 1862 on St. Cloud Hill, south of the city center.

But that rapid effort was costly. Fort Negley owes its existence to the 2,768 men who helped to construct it. Most of the men were Black, some free and some enslaved, who were pressed into service by the Union Army. These men felled trees, hauled earth, and cut and laid limestone for the fort. They slept out in the open and enjoyed few, if any, comforts while they labored. Between 600 and 800 men died while building the fort, and in total only 310 received payment for their work. Fort Negley was abandoned by the military after the war, and over the years it has gone through cycles of neglect and restoration.

▲ Fort Negley

▲ Fort Negley

All of this history is yours for the learning when you visit the fort. After driving through the stone archway at the park's entrance, head to the visitors center, the best place to start on your first visit. Inside, a small museum offers interactive exhibits detailing the work done by the fort's laborers, as well as Nashville's role in the Civil War. For an even deeper dive, you can make an appointment to see the museum's collection of Civil War artifacts, including letters dated from 1858 to 1865.

For all the academic stimulation indoors, it was the outside that finally had me adding Fort Negley as one of my regular haunts. The nearly 60-acre site includes a paved loop trail around the base of the fort and raised boardwalks that cut through the fortifications. Historical markers tell the story of the fort's construction and detail its military features. In spring, wildflowers like Queen Anne's lace and black-eyed Susans bloom on the hillside. A flat, grassy area at the top of the hill is a splendid picnic destination.

Best of all, Fort Negley's elevated location means it offers a unique view of Music City. Yes, lots of downtown skyscrapers boast cool perspectives, but Fort Negley's vantage point means you get a bird's-eye view of parts of the city you don't normally get to see. My favorite view looks to the southeast, over City Cemetery and 4th Avenue South. It's not packed with neon signs like you see from atop the downtown hotels, but instead it's a peek at a peaceful city neighborhood. If you look to the north, you can take in the downtown skyline and the Batman Building; this is a fun vista, but it's something you can see elsewhere.

The fort is run by the Metro Nashville Parks Department, which means it's free and open to the public. The total distance of the park's paths is less than a mile. The exterior paths are wheelchair accessible; some of the interior paths have staircases or are not accessible because they are in need of repair. There are some modest slopes on the uphill climb. Dogs and strollers are welcome. Heed signage and make a donation in the visitors center if you'd like to help preserve this historic park.

Connect with...

㉒ Get the best views of the city
㊲ Lace up your boots for an urban hike

11 Snack, shop, and swim on Dickerson Pike

Neighborhoods and City Streets • Food • Shopping

Why Go: Dickerson Pike is an unexpected treasure trove of history and community that feels like it's for locals only.

Where: Starting point: Buffalo Park, where Dickerson Pike meets N. 1st St., 2 miles northeast of downtown. Dickerson Pike continues north from there; the attractions covered here span about 2 miles. It's a walkable distance, but you could also go by bike or car.

Timing: Head this way during the summer, when you can spend a hot day soaking in the pool at the Dive Motel and Swim Club, and a warm night sipping an icy cocktail or two.

In the 1950s and 1960s, Dickerson Pike was dotted with motels, which were popular with musicians in town on tour or looking for a place to party (often poolside). Big names like Hank Williams Jr. and James Brown would drink beer and have a good time. Nashville's economy soon changed, though, and so did Dickerson Pike. For years this area had a high-crime rate and wasn't a draw for locals or tourists, despite its history and proximity to downtown and the interstates. Today, Dickerson Pike is undergoing a revitalization. Alongside the well-established tire shops and car dealerships are startups and other small businesses, a number of which are BIPOC-owned. The mixture of old and new results in a vibe that's a little grittier and more eclectic than elsewhere in Nashville.

Start your exploration where Dickerson Pike meets North 1st Street in a small, triangular-shaped patch of land alongside I-24. This is called **Buffalo Park,** but it's more like a grassy median. The park's name is a reference to the route that Dickerson Pike now follows: the Buffalo Trace. This path was tamped down by bison hooves, as the large mammals made their way from salt licks north of town to the banks of the Cumberland River. You're welcome to get up close and personal with the park's large bronze bison sculptures, but to do so you'll need to

Coneheads

Buffalo Park

cross a busy section of Dickerson Pike. Park on a side street and walk over or stay at a distance on the sidewalk and use your zoom lens to snap a photo.

From here, head north for food, music, drinks, and more. First, stop and get a sugar high: The Black women-owned **Shugga Hi Bakery and Café** (1000 Dickerson Pike, 615/928-6576, www.shuggahibakeryandcafe.com) specializes in cakes and cookies. On the next block, **Drkmttr** (1111 Dickerson Pike, 615/669-1614, www.drkmttrcollective.com) is an all-ages, largely volunteer-run live music, theater, and event space. During 2020, when the coronavirus pandemic left many in need, Drkmttr opened a mutual-aid store and community refrigerator so that community members could procure (or donate) produce, meat, cleaning supplies, and other items.

Continue about a quarter mile north to admire custom- and locally made furnishings at **Good Wood Nashville** (1307 Dickerson Pike, 615/454-3817, https://goodwoodnashville. com). Peruse their handcrafted tables, shelving, and more. After the city was hit by devastating tornadoes in 2020, Good Wood created a series of "Nashville Strong" signs as a fundraiser for

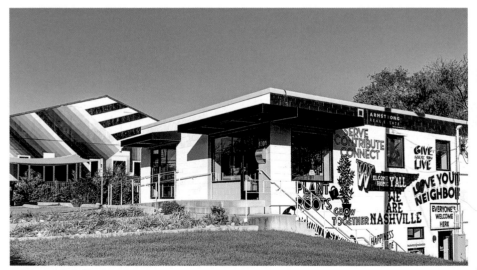

▲ Retrograde Coffee

local small businesses. Next, ponder your purchases at **Retrograde Coffee** (1305 Dickerson Pike, 615/964-7770, www.retrogradecoffee.com) next door, which serves pour-over and drip coffee and creates custom blends from beans across the globe. In summer, Retrograde hosts local farms that sell fresh produce and flowers in the parking lot.

When you're hungry, **Coneheads** (1315 Dickerson Pike, 629/888-4967, www.conehead-scw.com) is a few storefronts north. Former Vanderbilt University linebacker Marcus Buggs made a twist on the southern classic—chicken and waffles—by putting the chicken inside a waffle cone. Top it with a "cap" of coleslaw and eat while you walk.

The **Dive Motel and Swim Club** (1414 Dickerson Pike, 615/650-9103, www.thedivemotel.com) has garnered much attention since its 2019 opening. This spot was once the Key Motel, one of the street's beloved party spots from the 1960s. Today, it's a revamped lodging with a disco ball in every room. But it's locals, not tourists, who flock here: A day pass or membership allows you to hang out by the Instagram-worthy pool and drink at the hotel bar, one of the hippest places in town to see and be seen.

End your time on Dickerson with a taco from **Taqueria Andrea and La Mini Michoacana** (1605 Dickerson Pike, 615/678-1151), which serves house-made Salvadoran, Honduran, and Mexican favorites as well as more than 25 varieties of fresh *paletas* (fruit popsicles), fanned out in an overwhelmingly colorful display.

Connect with...

4 Shop local in East Nashville

8 Scope out vintage gems on Gallatin Pike

12 Go backstage at the Ryman Auditorium

Only in Nashville • Be a Tourist in Your City

Why Go: There's no place in American music as storied as the historic Ryman Auditorium. It's great to see a live show here, but taking the backstage tour lets you in on lots of little secrets and some awesome photo ops.

Where: Downtown, half a block north of Broadway • 116 Rep. John Lewis Way/5th Ave. N., https://ryman.com/tours/backstage • $25-35 adults, $17-30 children

Timing: Self-guided tours take place during the day. Set aside about an hour and go on a weekday when there's not a major event or festival in town. That way, you'll have plenty of elbow room and time to take in all the details. The 40-minute guided tours are offered after a live show (on nights with only one show). For a guided tour, you'll need a ticket to that night's show, plus a tour ticket.

I can't remember how many shows I've seen at the Ryman. (On a few memorable weekends, I went to three shows back-to-back-to-back, so it's a big number.) Of all these shows, nearly every artist took a moment to note how powerful it was to play that stage. Standing where so many other influential musicians have stood, having their voice resonate through the Ryman's hallowed halls—it's a big moment. Even the most jaded musicians are known to get teary-eyed when they step onstage. Witnessing that emotion makes you want to understand what makes this place so special. And the best way to do that is by taking one of the Ryman's backstage tours.

▲ Ryman Auditorium entrance

There are two options: the self-guided tour during the day and the guided tour after a show. On both tours, you'll go backstage and see hallways bedecked with signed concert posters and historic photographs and walk through the themed dressing rooms. The tours cover the same information, but each has its own appeal: The guided tours offer you the opportunity to ask questions as you ride the buzz of having just seen a show, while the self-guided tours allow for a more leisurely pace to examine all the ephemera on the walls.

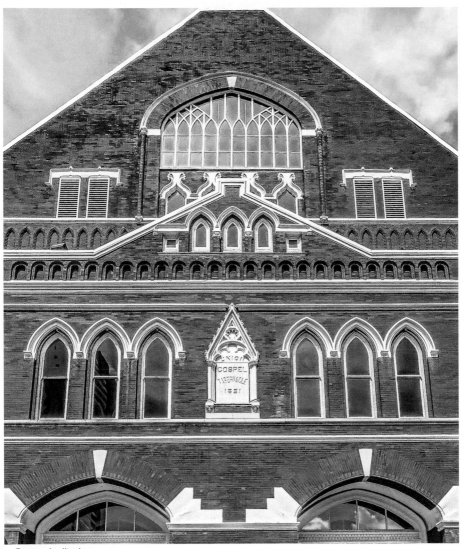

Ryman Auditorium

On the guided tour you'll hear a lot of tales—from funny to unbelievable—of your favorite stars over the years. But first, a short video starts things off by explaining the Ryman's important role in Nashville's history. In 1892, Captain Thomas Ryman built the Union Gospel Tabernacle as a venue for the charismatic preaching of Reverend Samuel P. Jones. Ryman had a religious awakening at a revival led by Jones and wanted to give him an appropriate space to preach to others. Over the decades, the Ryman hosted performers of all kinds. Harry Houdini even did his magic here in 1924.

In 1943, the brick building with excellent acoustics became the home of a popular barn dance called the Grand Ole Opry. In 1956, June Carter was singing backup vocals at the Ryman for Elvis Presley. She met Johnny Cash backstage, and the rest is history. Stained glass was added to the building's arched windows in 1966. After the Opry left in 1974, the Ryman fell into disrepair and was almost condemned until Gaylord Entertainment, the company that owns the Opry, brought the Mother Church of Country Music back to its former glory, complete with pew-style seats that can accommodate nearly 2,500 people.

In its early days, the Ryman didn't have dressing rooms for its performers. Maude Adams almost backed out of her gig at the Ryman in 1932 because of this; that's when the first make-shift room was cobbled together. Today there are nine dressing rooms backstage, each with a theme and named after stars who helped make the place famous, like Minnie Pearl and Roy Acuff. On the tours you'll be able to go inside them, perch at a vanity, and see what it feels like to be a star like Margo Price getting ready to go onstage, examining your reflection in a mirror framed with lights. The backstage tour also includes plenty of museum-style exhibits about the musicians who have performed here through the ages, complete with instruments, sheet music, and costumes.

The Ryman is sought out by performers, thanks to its intimate nature and its near-perfect acoustics. You can whisper onstage, and—without the aid of a microphone or speakers—be heard throughout the audience. Ketch Secor of the band Old Crow Medicine Show describes the Ryman this way: "It is like the room itself is an instrument." Just like the sound from a guitar or banjo resonates when the instrument is played, so, too, does the Ryman Auditorium when musicians get onstage. So, perhaps the best moment of the tour is getting to walk on that

Local Lore

Because the Ryman was originally built as a church, it didn't have the backstage green rooms that you'd expect of a venue of its ilk. When it was home to the Grand Ole Opry between 1943 and 1972, stars waiting to go onstage would do so at the honky-tonks on the north side of Broadway. These spots backed up to an alley, across which was the side entrance to the Ryman. When it was time to go on, someone would call out from the Ryman's side door, and the performers would hustle across the alley. The Opry stars could reliably make it from the bars to the stage in time for their curtain call. Today, most of these honky-tonks still have back entrances, and several have second stages in the back, with different live music acts than in the front.

revered stage yourself. If you want, you can sing a line or two and see what it feels like to belt it out over the pews. Be sure to have your official souvenir photo taken to prove you were there.

Connect with...

7 Kick up your heels at a honky-tonk

17 Hear up-and-coming musicians first

48 Trace the origins of country music to Bristol

13 Relive the Nashville sit-ins
at the Civil Rights Room

Only in Nashville • Black Heritage

Why Go: The Nashville sit-ins were vital in desegregation efforts in the city and nationwide. Learning about the city's role in this watershed time is essential for understanding the Civil Rights Movement.

Where: Nashville Public Library, 615 Church St., 615/862-5782, http://library.nashville.org • 9am-6pm Mon.-Sat., 2pm-5pm Sun. • free

Timing: The Civil Rights Room is open when the library is open. If you want to take a staff-led tour of the exhibit, request it online at least two weeks in advance.

Inside the main branch of the Nashville Public Library is a moving homage to one of the city's most defining, historic moments. The second floor houses a powerful freestanding exhibit,

▲ Civil Rights Room

almost a mini museum, centered around the sit-ins of the Civil Rights Movement of the 1950s and 1960s. The library is a fitting location for the collection: It's part of the neighborhood that was the epicenter of the Nashville sit-ins during the 1960s.

In 1959, Nashville was a racially segregated city. A group of students from Nashville's historically Black colleges and universities—Fisk, Meharry, American Baptist, and Tennessee A&I—as well as some from Vanderbilt University formed the Nashville Student Movement. They organized to enter retail stores downtown and sit at the segregated lunch counters, where Black people were not permitted to eat. Some of the stores put up "closed" signs; all refused to serve the Black students. For the next three months, the students sat. They wanted to draw attention to the racial injustice of segregation as well as the economic power of Black customers.

While the protests that took place in Nashville are categorized as nonviolent because the student protestors did not engage in violence, it's important to remember that the reaction to the protests was often aggressive, even violent. White segregationists hurled insults and tried

▲ lunch counter exhibit at the Civil Rights Room

▲ Woolworth on Fifth

to dislodge the Black protestors, spitting in their faces, punching them, and even extinguishing cigarettes on their skin. On February 27, 1960, white attackers physically pulled some students off their seats and onto the ground. Police arrested 73 students that day, including a young John Lewis. None of the attackers were arrested. It took until May 1960 for Nashville's mayor and the stores to agree to serve Black customers at the lunch counters. And while Nashville was the first Southern city to desegregate public services, other types of segregation continued until the passage of the Civil Rights Act of 1964.

Today, the Nashville sit-ins and the people who worked for desegregation are honored in the **Civil Rights Room** at the library. The focal element of the exhibit is a circular table, representing one of the lunch counters where the members of the Nashville Student Movement sat. Take a seat at one of the stools surrounding the counter and read the engravings there: These are the 10 rules of conduct that were set out for sit-in participants, including: "Be polite and courteous at all times, regardless of how you are treated." A timeline of the events of the Civil Rights Movement, both in Nashville and nationwide, is presented atop the table.

The Civil Rights Room is ringed by nearly life-sized black-and-white photographs depicting major events in Nashville, including a school desegregation, sit-ins, and a silent march to the courthouse. You'll even see John Lewis's mugshot from one of his arrests. Inside a glass-enclosed viewing room, you can choose from six different documentary videos, including an hour-long 1960 NBC news documentary about the sit-ins. Many of the videos are 30 minutes or longer, so plan on spending several hours here if you want to see all of them.

Before you leave, take a moment to absorb the quote from Martin Luther King Jr., who gave a speech at Fisk University in 1960. A large glass inscription reads, "I came to Nashville not to bring inspiration, but to gain inspiration from the great movement that has taken place in this community."

There are other places around town that honor the Civil Rights Movement. Just a few blocks from the library, you can see where some of the sit-ins happened by walking up Rep. John Lewis Way (renamed from 5th Avenue in 2021 in honor of the late activist and U.S. Representative). In 2018, **Woolworth on Fifth** (221 Rep. John Lewis Way/5th Ave. N.) was opened as a Southern restaurant, featuring a recreated lunch counter with many of the original fixtures from the Woolworth drugstore where the sit-ins took place. The restaurant has since closed and is being turned into a small theater. For now, it's worth peering through the window at the lunch counter.

The *Tennessee Transforms* exhibit at the **Tennessee State Museum** (1000 Rosa Parks Blvd., 615/741-2692, www.tn.gov/museum) covers the acts of resistance statewide, not just in Nashville. Stop in this free museum to see reproductions of the segregation signs Black patrons faced, more historic sit-in photography and videos, and artifacts from Green Book hotels that welcomed Black travelers.

Nashville's **Witness Walls** (1 Public Sq., www.metroartsnashville.com/witness-walls) are public sculptures outside of the Davidson County Courthouse (to which protestors marched in 1960). Designed by Walter Hood, these concrete walls feature friezes of the names of protestors and images of that tumultuous time in Nashville history.

Connect with...

6 Celebrate Black culture and history on Jefferson Street

16 Get collegiate in the Athens of the South

25 Feed your mind in North Nashville

14 Learn to two-step or line dance

Only in Nashville • Live Music

Why Go: Is there anything more Nashville than boot-scooting? But it doesn't come naturally to everyone. If you need to brush up your skills or are starting from scratch, take a dance lesson—then get out on the floor.

Where: Many bars and live music venues offer free dance lessons. These take place across town, but are concentrated in East Nashville, downtown, and Music Valley.

Timing: Many classes take place in the early evening before the live music starts and last less than an hour. If you really want to perfect your skills, plan to go back regularly. Practice makes perfect.

You know a good time is imminent when the tables and chairs in front of a stage are rearranged to make room for dancing. If you've always been too intimidated to join in, then take advantage of the many free and low-cost dance lessons around town. If you have a partner, bring one. If not, you can practice with other folks who may soon be friends (line dancing doesn't require a partner). Wear clothes in which you can move and be comfortable and know that cowboy boots are never out of place. Bring cash to tip your instructors and plan to buy a drink or two from the businesses that make this fun available.

While it's more than 10 miles away from the honky-tonks on Broadway, **Nashville Palace** (2611 McGavock Pl., 615/889-1541) in Music Valley is a local favorite for authentic country western music, offering free dance lessons many nights a week. The restaurant and bar is festooned with country music-themed decor (including a giant guitar fashioned from string lights on the ceiling). It's a big space with multiple stages, so one room might feature Western swing and two-step lessons while another has you learning line dances.

Honky Tonk Tuesday Nights at the **American Legion 82** (3204 Gallatin Pike, 615/228-3598) is one of the most fun nights out in Music City. Once a week, The Cowpokes, the house band, take the stage in full western garb and transform a standard, under-the-radar American Legion post into a multigenerational party. Before the show starts, you can get some

The Five Spot

Nashville Palace

instruction on how to do the two-step from Laura Mae Socks. She'll teach you the basics, which you can use later on the dance floor. Bring cash to tip the band and your dance teacher—and so you can partake of the $3 beers. The crowd is a mix of neighborhood residents, AL regulars, and young, hip folks who want to dance. If you want to wear a snap-front shirt and boots, you won't be out of place, but a t-shirt and jeans will work, too.

Monday nights are all about **The Five Spot** (1006 Forrest Ave., 615/650-9333) in East Nashville. This bar, which often appeared in the TV show *Nashville,* is welcoming to all kinds of dance moves. The club's **Motown Mondays** features Electric Western, a DJ team that plays doo wop, girl groups, and other classic tunes from the 1950s and '60s. At the beginning of the evening there are free dance lessons so you can learn some swing steps in advance. You don't need to bring a partner to join in. The lessons are free but remember to buy a drink or two at the bar and tip your servers and teachers. The crowd here is young and tends to dress up, so you may want to swing by **High Class Hillbilly** (4604 Gallatin Pike, http://highclasshillbilly.com) first for some vintage duds to complete your look.

▲ Wildhorse Saloon

There's less line dancing in Music City than the movies would have you think. But if you want to learn how, **Wildhorse Saloon** (120 2nd Ave. N., 615/902-8200, http://wildhorsesaloon.com) is the place to do it. Owned by Ryman Hospitality, which also owns the Grand Ole Opry, Wildhorse Saloon claims to be the largest restaurant per capita in the state. It boasts three floors, live music, food, and free line dancing lessons throughout the day and night. There will be lots of hooting and hollering and you'll be forward shuffling with lots of folks from out of town. It's easy to show up solo and start moving. Boots are optional but recommended.

Line dancing lessons are available at pop-up spots across the city thanks to **New Boots Line Dancing** (613 Ewing Ave., 629/777-6086, www.newbootslinedancing.com). Multiple classes for groups of up to 25 people are offered on the weekends, so you're likely to find a slot that you can join and meet some new friends as you all move one step forward and two steps back. You can also gather a group of your besties and schedule a private lesson. After class, you'll even get a video of your group's last dance as a souvenir.

If you prefer to dance to the beat of a different genre, you can still get moving at **Plaza Mariachi** (3955 Nolensville Pike, 615/373-9292, http://plazamariachi.com), a seven-day-a-week celebration. At their regular free salsa dancing classes, you can learn all the moves and then stick around to dance to house mariachi bands. You can also watch aerial silk dancers perform their jaw-dropping moves—a different skill set entirely.

Connect with...

7 Kick up your heels at a honky-tonk
18 Celebrate Latin America at Plaza Mariachi

15 Create a masterpiece at a makerspace

Why Go: Get your creative juices flowing by seeing what other artists are doing at studios around town, then book a workshop or class at a makerspace to get in on the action.

Where: Just as there's a music studio in nearly every neighborhood in Nashville, there's also likely a makerspace tucked away somewhere. Wedgewood-Houston, 1.5 miles south of downtown, has a concentration of creative spaces and galleries where you can get your hands dirty.

Timing: Afternoon is a good time to see artists at work in their studios. Visit a few galleries at once during events like the **Wedgewood-Houston Art Crawl** (www.we-hoartsnashville.com), which takes place on the first Saturday of the month. There are also art crawls in East Nashville, downtown, and Germantown. Makerspace schedules vary by location.

Nashville is more than just musicians and songwriters. The city's creative essence makes visual artists feel at home here, too. If you want to get in on the creative process, you can visit artists' studios and makerspaces. Many offer workshops and classes that cover technique in different disciplines, allowing you to dabble in just about any creative endeavor out there.

There's no single sculptor who has become more iconic in Nashville than Alan LeQuire. Among his head-turners in the city are *Musica,* a jumble of joyous human figures in the Music Row roundabout; *Athena,* the massive golden goddess at the Parthenon, and *Tennessee Woman Suffrage Monument,* a bronze depiction of five important people in the local women's suffrage movement. His Sylvan Park **LeQuire Gallery** (4304 Charlotte Ave., 615/298-4611, www.le-quiregallery.com) features studies of these works and more original pieces, plus the work of other sculptors and painters. The gallery also offers classes and workshops, some of which are taught by LeQuire himself, and focus on working with clay and sculpting the human form.

As a child, Danielle McDaniel took her first pottery class through Nashville Metro Parks and Recreation. Now, as an adult, she's made it her mission to make ceramics available to

▵ LeQuire Gallery

▵ artist Dean Dixon at LeQuire Gallery

▵ Clay Lady's Campus

first-timers as well as professional artists, and everyone in between with **Clay Lady's Campus** (1416 Lebanon Pike, 615/242-03546, www.theclaylady.com). Sign up for one-day workshops or ongoing classes. As you sit at the pottery wheel and throw your first pots, you'll be surrounded by the creations of experienced artists, so you'll have plenty of inspiration. Also on-site is **Mid-South Ceramic** (615/242-0300, www.midsouthceramics.com), a pottery supply company.

A volunteer-run nonprofit makerspace in East Nashville, **Make Nashville** (620 Davidson St., 615/450-6253, http://makenashville.org) has a metal shop, ceramics studio, and welding, electronics, and 3D fabrication areas. The different disciplines each have their own space (you don't want sawdust on your electronics, after all), but the rooms are open enough that you can see what others are working on. The industrial space is functional and well-organized. And fittingly for Nashville, there are audio rooms for recording music and podcasts. In addition to classes and memberships (which allow access to all the tools on-site), Make Nashville also hosts maker faires, where you can buy goods created by local artisans.

▲ Turnip Green Creative Reuse

Other galleries and makerspaces are concentrated in the Wedgewood-Houston neighborhood, south of downtown: The offerings at the non-profit **Fort Houston Artisan Support Project** (217 Willow, 615/730-8865, www.forthoustonartisansupportproject.org) include a woodshop, printshop, and photo studio for those who make their living by creating beautiful things. Become a member to gain access to the equipment and work in the warehouse-like space. Fort Houston offers ongoing classes taught by artists in the community for all members of the public. It also supports the on-site **Gallery at Fort Houston,** which displays the work of local artists. Exhibitions change often and can be seen at the Wedgewood-Houston Art Crawl, as well as by appointment.

Folks in town donate fabric, markers, wallpaper, tile, paper, and other materials to **Turnip Green Creative Reuse** (407 Houston St., 615/720-7480, www.turnipgreencreativereuse.org) and the nonprofit sorts it and sells it back to people looking to make art. Spend some time looking through the abundant, well-organized bins and shelves to find affordable supplies—or inspiration for your next project. Proceeds from every purchase are used to teach art in local schools. Turnip Green also hosts hands-on workshops and classes on topics like plant propagation, mosaics, and sewing. A small area of the space is a gallery displaying the work of artists who have connections to Turnip Green.

At the volunteer-run **Coop Curatorial Collective** (507 Hagen St., www.coopgallery.org), the clean white walls are similar to that of other galleries—allowing for the works to shine in a neutral space—but the pieces are not. Expect to find art in a range of media, including digital, that will challenge you to think differently. The focus here is on the works and their message, not the retail component that's typical of most galleries. Members of the collective also help arrange collaborative shows with other exhibition spaces in town.

Connect with...

32 Get hands-on at kid-friendly museums
35 Wander the Buchanan Arts District

16 Get collegiate in the Athens of the South

Art and Culture • Only in Nashville

Why Go: Nashville's original nickname is more than a catchy moniker. Explore some of the sites that show the city's commitment to higher education, past and present.

Where: The Parthenon and the campuses covered here are all west of downtown, spanning from TSU in the north down to Belmont University.

Timing: Pick a temperate day for a stroll through the city's park-like campuses. They are more crowded in spring and fall and sleepier in summer.

Before Nashville was Nash Vegas, and even before it was Music City, it was the Athens of the South. The use of the term was popularized by Philip Lindsley, a Princeton-trained professor who moved to Nashville in 1824 to lead Cumberland College (later the University of Nashville). That was a full 47 years before Queen Victoria first coined the nickname "Music City."

Lindsley felt Nashville could emulate Athens, Greece, as a center of higher education. He wanted the University of Nashville to become nationally known and for the city's schools to offer education to people regardless of their economic status. He also helped normalize the idea that teachers needed specialized training to educate their students. Between 1866 and 1891, Fisk, Vanderbilt, Belmont, and Lipscomb Universities were founded and Lindsley's vision became a reality. Today, there are more than 20 four-year colleges, universities, and community colleges in the city and its suburbs. Among them are religious universities, historically Black colleges and universities (HBCUs), design schools, and a member of the NCAA's Southeastern Conference (SEC).

In 1897, Nashville wanted to play up its reputation as the Athens of the South even more. As part of an exposition celebrating Tennessee's centennial, the city built a life-size replica of **The Parthenon** (2500 West End Ave., 615/862-8431, www.nashvilleparthenon.com), the many-columned Athenian temple. By the 1920s, the original wood-and-plaster structure was crumbling, so the city had it rebuilt using tinted concrete. The structure still stands, an iconic

Vanderbilt University

The Parthenon

Belmont University

landmark. During the day, you can walk up and down the steps to appreciate its mammoth size, then go inside to see its three gallery spaces and the 42-foot statue of the goddess Athena, by local sculptor Alan LeQuire. The Parthenon is most beautiful from the outside, particularly when it's lit up at night.

You don't have to be a student or faculty member to enjoy Nashville's colleges. In addition to their scenic campuses, many offer programs for those who just like to learn.

Just across West End Avenue from The Parthenon is **Vanderbilt University** (2201 West End Ave., 615/322-7311, www.vanderbilt.edu), named for Commodore Cornelius Vanderbilt, who donated $1 million in 1873 to found a university that he hoped would connect different populations of the country. When I first stepped on this campus, dotted with brick buildings and fragrant blooming magnolia trees, I thought it looked like a dollhouse version of a college—picture perfect. The entire campus is an arboretum, with more than 190 different species of plants, including the 200-year-old Bicentennial Oak, which predates the school. The oak is east of the Sarratt Student Center near the Old Central building. (A full arboretum map is available online.) The campus also houses two art galleries. **Sarratt Gallery** (2301 Vanderbilt Pl., 615/322-2425, www.vanderbilt.edu/sarrattgallery) is in the main student center and exhibits work by alumni and students. The **Vanderbilt University Fine Arts Gallery** (1220 21st Ave. S., 615/322-0605, www.library.vanderbilt.edu/gallery) has a wide-ranging collection, covering nearly every region of the world.

On the east side of Hillsboro Village is **Belmont University** (1900 Belmont Blvd., 615/460-6000, www.belmont.edu). Founded as a school for girls in 1890, the school went through several iterations before becoming a higher-education institution in 1991. The tidy main campus is ringed with red brick buildings and magnolia trees that frame green quads. Stop in the **Gallery of Iconic Guitars** (1907 Belmont Blvd., 615/460-6984, www.thegigat-belmont.com), which boasts a collection of the stringed instruments dating from 1890 to 1950. Also on campus is the large **Belmont Mansion** (1900 Belmont Blvd.), which was constructed in 1853 by enslaved people. Check the schedule of the **Curb Event Center** (2002 Belmont Blvd.), which hosts sporting events, concerts, and lectures.

Close to Belmont is the **Scarritt Bennett Center** (1027 18th Ave. S., 615/340-7500, http://scarrittbennett.org), once the campus for the Scarritt College for Christian Workers. Today, the Gothic Revival buildings house a nonprofit center focused on economic empowerment and social justice. Head to the corner of the campus near 19th Avenue South and Grand Avenue for a meditative walk in the labyrinth of the International Peace Garden.

Nashville is also home to four historically Black colleges: Fisk University, Meharry Medical College, American Baptist College, and Tennessee State University. To best experience Fisk's cultural heritage, visit on **Jubilee Day.** Across the street from Fisk is **Meharry Medical College** (1005 Dr. D. B. Todd Jr. Blvd., 615/327-6000, https://home.mmc.edu), which opened in 1915 as the first medical school for African Americans in the South. Meharry also includes Nashville General, the city's public hospital.

The main campus of **Tennessee State University** (3500 John A Merritt Blvd., www.tnstate.edu) occupies 500 acres to the west of Fisk and Meharry, bumping up against the banks of the Cumberland River to the north. Attractions include the imposing semicircular brick performing arts center and Hale Stadium, also known as "The Hole," built in 1953. The Tigers now play football at Nissan Stadium downtown, but other events are hosted at The Hole.

In the Athens of the South, education comes first, so there are plenty of places eager to teach you, whether you're a prospective student, a lifelong learner, or you just want to while away a day in a picturesque setting.

Connect with...

- **3** Hear sweet music on Jubilee Day
- **25** Feed your mind in North Nashville
- **33** Lunch at an old-timer restaurant

17 Hear up-and-coming musicians first

Why Go: Catch talented musicians before they get to the rhinestones-and-sold-out-venues stage of their careers. Because there's nothing better than being able to say, "I saw that band play in a little club before anyone had heard of them."

Where: Most of these smaller venues are in SoBro (the area just south of Broadway), plus a couple of must-visits in Midtown and East Nashville.

Timing: Most venues have shows several times a week, including some weekend brunch and early evening shows, as well as the more typical evening slots. An afternoon gig might last less than an hour, but most evening shows are around two hours.

Nashville is home to big-name stars. It's not unusual to see Ben Folds around Music Row, spot Nicole Kidman or Keith Urban at the library, or run into Brad Paisley and Kimberly Williams Paisley at The Store, their no-cost shop to fight food insecurity. But Nashville's real power, its charm, its buzz, comes from its up-and-coming musicians. The folks who hope to—and are about to—hit it big. Sometimes they're on the stage of the Ryman or at the Grand Ole Opry, making an appearance with a big-name friend or working as a session musician. But more often they're playing an intimate venue—so your only job is to find them. Here are some of my favorite venues, where I go when I want to step away from the honky-tonks and the Opry and hear a different Nashville melody. Most of these spots are all-ages at least some of the time, so you can take kids on your musical exploration.

You won't necessarily recognize the names on the lineup at **The Listening Room Cafe** (618 4th Ave. S., 615/259-3600, http://listeningroomcafe.com), but pay attention, as you're likely catching the next hitmaker. Unlike at a typical listening room, there are no rules against conversation, but the idea is to come to hear the performers, not your friends. This SoBro venue has a full menu and bar, including a popular brunch, during which you'll be serenaded by local singer-songwriters (plus the occasional national act). Large tables make this venue popular with groups, as well as those with folks under 21 in their group.

Marathon Music Works

Marathon Music Works

The Listening Room Cafe

The neighborhood bar and grill **3rd and Lindsley** (818 3rd Ave. S., 615/259-9891, www.3rdandlindsley.com) has some of the best bookers in town lining up rock, alternative, progressive, Americana, soul, and R&B performances. If you were just passing by, you wouldn't think a place that rocks could reside inside; it looks more like the DMV than a place where you want to spend late nights. But Monday nights feature The Time Jumpers, a world-class Western swing jam band that occasionally includes Vince Gill. The club offers good sound quality and an adequate dance floor and seating. The atmosphere isn't particularly quirky or cozy, but you came here for music, not decor.

Housed at the historic Marathon Village, **Marathon Music Works** (1402 Clinton St., 615/891-1781, www.marathonmusicworks.com) is one of the city's non-country-music standouts. The building, an early 1900s auto factory, is now a brick-lined music venue with high ceilings, several bars, and an interior space that is modified depending on the vibe of the show. It's usually standing room only with space to dance, but seating, VIP areas, and extra bar areas may be added. Acts run the gamut from dance music to rock to rap. Rapper Struggle Jennings, the step-grandson of Waylon Jennings, is the closest to a country act that's played here in recent memory. Marathon Village is also home to a distillery, restaurants, and bars, making it an easy place to spend a night on the town.

Few people had as much to do with underscoring Nashville's reputation as a music town—not just a country-music town—as Jack White. The rocker opened his Nashville outpost of **Third Man Records** (623 7th Ave. S., 615/891-4393, http://thirdmanrecords.com) in 2009, and since then the combination record store and music venue has been a magnet for live shows, including Billie Eilish, the North Mississippi Allstars, and many acts that are not household names—yet. The lineup is reliably offbeat, and heavily skewed to indie rock. The annual Record Store Day in April is a particularly good time to catch a show at Third Man, but there's no need to wait for a special occasion. Many of the employees are in bands themselves, so you might come across an impromptu show while you're browsing the vinyl here. They can tell you what's going on elsewhere around town, too.

Mike Grimes is responsible for three of Nashville's favorite spots for live music. **Grimey's New and Pre-Loved Music** (1060 E. Trinity Ln., 615/226-3811, www.grimeys.com) is a record shop that hosts free local shows timed with the release of the performers' albums. (The building's exterior walls are even painted with murals depicting new album covers.) Sometimes nationally known artists perform here, and you'll find the store's aisles as packed as any mosh pit. Grimey's has an air of possibility about it: You never know who might pop in for a short set. Grimes's other two establishments are siblings: **The Basement East** (917 Woodland St., 615/645-9174, www.thebasementnashville.com) has only been around since 2015, but it's just as beloved as **The Basement** (1604 8th Ave. S.). Both venues book local bands and host new music nights. The 475-person-capacity Basement East (locals call it "The Beast") and The Basement both have outdoor space, but the bulk of the action goes on inside, where you might catch a singer-songwriter one night and a heavy metal band the next. The Basement describes itself as "a cellarful of noise," and in some ways it's true. The small, brick-walled space is literally in the basement of a building. Going to a show here feels like listening to your friends play music in a neighbor's cellar...if your friends were really talented.

Connect with...

① Try your hand at songwriting

㉔ Strum and pick your way through local guitar shops

㉖ Rhapsodize about your favorites at music museums

18 Celebrate Latin America at Plaza Mariachi

Live Music • Families and Kids • Food

Why Go: It's hard to be in a bad mood at Plaza Mariachi, a giant Latin American marketplace filled with food, music, art, and joy.

Where: 7 miles south of downtown • 3955 Nolensville Pike, 615/373-9292, www.plazamariachi.com • 11am-8pm Sun.-Mon., 11am-9pm Tues.-Thurs., 11am-10pm Fri.-Sat. • free to visit; individual merchant and concert prices vary

Timing: Plan to hang out for a few hours. Eat some food, take a dance lesson, listen to the band, and shop for some treats to go. Because Plaza Mariachi is in a former grocery store, there are few windows. With its colored lights and decor designed to make it feel like you're outdoors, Plaza Mariachi is like a casino or cruise ship, in that it is very easy to lose track of time. Come for a taco and a pan dulce, leave three hours later after a margarita and learning to salsa.

Plaza Mariachi is a former Kroger grocery store in a strip mall that's been turned into a 70,000-square-foot gathering place for Nashville's Latinx community, as well as a destination for people of all backgrounds looking for food, music, and fun in a buzzing venue. The retrofit space is a facsimile of a Mexican neighborhood, complete with archways, street lamps, tile work, and original art. Each of the five internal "streets" are adorned with small businesses just like you'd find in town, including clothing boutiques, bakeries and restaurants, a grocery store, art galleries, an arcade, and even a spa. Many of the individual business owners in the complex are Latinx.

The centerpiece is the indoor plaza, where people are as friendly as they were on the classic TV show *Villa Alegre,* and where, surprisingly, they burst into song just as often. Almost any time of day, you'll encounter some kind of performance: live music, like a mariachi band playing a call-and-response; other live bands from nationally known singers to local pop groups; aerial performers hanging from silks swaying to DJ music; or salsa dancers. The vibe is cross-cultural: You'll know you're in Tennessee when you hear the mariachi band play that local classic "Rocky Top" as they roam the corridors.

one of the streets in Plaza Mariachi

cultural dance performance

aerial silks performers

93

▲ performers dancing outside of Plaza Mariachi

You'll find kids running up and down the halls and dancing to the beat, particularly at lunchtime. Kid-centric activities include face painting, story time, and an indoor playground and arcade; check the website for listings for the week. For the grown-ups, weekend evenings give the plaza a nightclub vibe, and the partying lasts well past midnight, with neon flashing lights, loud laughter, and a few drinks. The soundtrack may be live or DJ dance music, or even a film that encourages audience participation.

Show up hungry, because there are plenty of places to feast, thanks to the food court with a number of different Latin American restaurants. Have a full meal at Argentinean steak house **Tres Gauchos** or made-to-order tacos at **Taqueria Hidalgo,** or head to **El Ceviche Loco,** a walk-up ceviche bar. Restaurants come and go in the space, but there are usually Cuban, Argentinean, Mexican, and Honduran spots, among other choices. No matter what I've eaten for lunch or dinner, I stop in **Mazfresco Market** before I leave to stock up on pan dulce from the bakery (full disclosure: I eat one in the car on the way home) and thick chocolate bars for making hot chocolate.

It's free to come hang out at Plaza Mariachi (there's even free Wi-Fi early in the day), and most of the music, the dance performances, and even the salsa lessons are free, although, in Nashville tradition, you ought to tip the musicians handsomely. There may be a charge for specific concerts and events. Parking is free and ample (even the former Kroger parking lot has been transformed with tile and landscaping).

Connect with...
㉗ Feast on Kurdish food
㊱ Taste the international flavors of Nolensville Pike

19 Shop and sip in The Nations

Neighborhoods and City Streets • Shopping

Why Go: Two fun pastimes—shopping and brewery-hopping—come together in this residential neighborhood that's pleasantly walkable.

Where: About 6 miles west of downtown, just north of I-40 • bounded by Charlotte Ave., 63rd Ave. N., Briley Pkwy., and Centennial Blvd • main strip: 51st Ave. N. • www.thenations615.com

Timing: An afternoon in The Nations is an ideal way to while away a few hours.

Shopping and beer-drinking are two pursuits that might not seem like they go together, but The Nations has evolved and expanded in the last few years, organically becoming a hub for both local microbreweries and small boutiques.

Like many other Nashville neighborhoods, The Nations was substantially changed by the flood of 2010. Many of the modest homes in this working-class neighborhood were damaged by the high water. Afterward, many residents moved out of the area; developers soon followed, adding new multistory homes and condo complexes to the existing mix of industrial buildings and original 1950s and '60s homes. Scattered throughout are boutiques, murals, coffee shops, bars, the city's only restaurant that is also a dog park, and arguably more microbreweries than anywhere else in Nashville. The best way to enjoy this neighborhood is to spend some time window-shopping and browsing its independent shops, then check out a brewery or two (or three).

Your shopping adventure should start at **Stocking 51** (5061 Centennial Blvd., http://stocking51.com), the head-turning former Belle Meade Hosiery Mill. Originally built in 1925, the brick structure has been renovated to add welcoming outdoor patios and is now home to stores, restaurants, and more. Inside you'll find women's leather shoes, clothing, and jewelry on the shelves at **ABLE** (5022 Centennial Blvd., 615/723-4836, www.livefashionable.com), a fashion brand that focuses on ethical products and paying a living wage. In fact, the company

15-story silo decorated with a massive mural by Guido Van Helten

publishes what they pay for the labor and goods that go into their products, offering complete transparency. Another star here is **Project 615** (1404 51st Ave. N., 615/428-0075, http://project615.com), known for iconic t-shirts that support local nonprofits (you've probably seen folks wearing the ones that say "Spread Love; It's the Nashville Way").

Across the street from Stocking 51, towering over the neighborhood, is a 15-story **silo** decorated with a massive **mural.** Painted by Guido Van Helten, it depicts long-time area resident Lee Estes. Estes grew up in the neighborhood—in the shadow of the silo—and watched as his face was painted larger than life on the mural. You can even see the silo from the interstate as you approach The Nations.

On the south side of I-40 on Charlotte Avenue are two other buildings, like Stocking 51, that are chock-full of small shops. **Sylvan Supply** (4101 Charlotte Ave., http://sylvansupply.com) is a former 1959 textile mill that's been redesigned to welcome shops like the well-curated **Woodland Wine Merchant** (615/712-8670, https://woodlandwinemerchant.com), restaurants, and outdoor space for lounging. Longtime locals once knew **L&L Market** (3820 Charlotte Ave., http://landlmarket.com) as a restaurant supply house. Today the mammoth brick building houses small boutiques, such as a **Made in TN gift shop** (615/419-7761, https://shopmadeintn.com), the well-lit **Amelia's Flowers** (615/712-7351, https://ameliasflowertruck.com), and lots of food purveyors.

The other main attraction in The Nations is to sample from the many taprooms and microbreweries in the area. **Fat Bottom Brewing** (800 44th Ave. N., 615/678-5715, http://fatbottombrewing.com) is known for its cross-section of beer styles, cheeky labels, local canned beers, and a large space for hanging out, tables for board games, outdoor areas, and more. You can look out at the brewery facility as you drink. At **51 North Taproom** (705 51st Ave. N., 629/800-2454, www.51northtaproom.com), there is a rotating selection of 30 beers and cider on tap, as well as more than 75 in cans and bottles. The cozy space has a full menu and is family-friendly. **Harding House Brewing Co.** (904 51st Ave. N., 615/678-1047, www.hardinghousebrew.com), which describes itself as a nano-brewery (meaning its production is even smaller than that of a microbrewery), focuses on using local ingredients in its beers. Inside Stocking 51, **Southern Grist** (5012 Centennial Blvd., 615/864-7133, www.southerngristbrewing.com), which was founded by three local couples, brews offbeat varieties of beer, like a coco-

⌃ Pennington Distilling Co.

nut IPA and a passionfruit sour. Most beers are small-batch and not around for very long. If you prefer your beverages with more punch, take a tour at **Pennington Distilling Co.** (900 44th Ave. N., 615/678-8986, http://penningtondistillingco.com), which makes small batch vodka and Tennessee whiskey.

Most of the taprooms serve food, but if you need more sustenance, there are plenty of places to grab a bite to eat, including **Daddy's Dogs** (5205 Centennial Blvd., 615/802-8481, http://daddysdogsnash.com), which has the feel of an old-fashioned drive-in. If you have your four-legged friend with you, stop at **El Paseo Nashville** (905 51st Ave. N., 615/866-9517, www.elpaseonashville.com), a Mexican restaurant with its own private outdoor dog park.

Connect with...

🔟 Get collegiate in the Athens of the South

㉕ Feed your mind in North Nashville

20 Embrace the kitsch at Madame Tussauds Wax Museum

Be a Tourist in Your City • Families and Kids

Why Go: Nashville's outpost of Madame Tussauds is the only one in the world that's themed around music.

Where: 11 miles northeast of downtown • 515 Opry Mills Dr., 615/485-4867, www.madametussauds.com/nashville • 10am-9pm Mon.-Sat., 11am-7pm Sun. • admission $19.99

Timing: A hot summer day is a good time to duck into some cool air-conditioning and take a deep dive into Nashville's music history. Allot an hour to 90 minutes to take it all in. The museum itself doesn't tend to get overly crowded, but the surrounding Opry Mills mall can, particularly during the Christmas season and on weekends.

As a small-town kid, I inhaled books about Europe at the turn of the century, and they would inevitably include Madame Tussaud and her wax museums. The concept of a museum full of wax versions of famous people always seemed fancy and glamorous to me—and also a little weird. In the nearly 200 years since Madame Tussaud's first museum opened in London, other outposts have opened all over the world, from Las Vegas to Tokyo. But it wasn't until one opened in Nashville that I got to see what I'd been reading about all those years ago.

I first went to Madame Tussaud's mostly for research. It seemed like something I might need to know about for a guidebook or when friends came to town, but I also went to satisfy my childhood fascination. I surprised myself after I left by texting friends while standing in the parking lot, including some lifelong Nashvillians, urging them to buy a ticket.

Located on the west side of the Opry Mills mall, the famous wax museum is chock-full of country music stars' likenesses and kitsch. But Nashville's Madame Tussauds isn't just a collection of lifelike statues—although they *are* remarkably lifelike, from the tattoos on Blake Shelton's arm to Justin Timberlake's stubble. The museum takes its theme of music seriously; its exhibits provide a chronology of modern music, largely from the 1950s to the present. You'll start by watching a film that summarizes the last five decades of American music history—and

Billie Holiday exhibit at Madame Tussauds Wax Museum

posing with a wax figure of Reba McEntire

▲ Tim McGraw exhibit

includes a good soundtrack. For the remainder of your visit, you'll wander through the museum's rooms, all populated with wax figures of some of the biggest music stars of every genre.

You'll experience a replica of WSM Radio, with its 1950s-era sound booth, old-fashioned microphone, and some classic country stars like George Jones. In October 1925, Nashville-based National Life and Accident Insurance Company opened a radio station in town. Its call letters stand for "We Shield Millions," the company's motto. This station started broadcasting the Grand Ole Opry in 1925, and that's still where you can hear the show today.

There's a room that's been fashioned into a nightclub playing rock music, for those who are burned out on country, where famous rockers like Ozzy Osbourne relax on velvet furnishings. There's also a replica of Nashville's RCA Studio B, with its cramped quarters and history-making piano. The real place is where Elvis Presley recorded more than 200 songs, so it's no surprise to encounter The King here.

This isn't the kind of museum where you have to stand a certain distance away from the exhibits. You can actually get up close and interact with the wax figures: Sing with them on

Historic Lore

During the French Revolution, in the late 1700s, Marie Tussaud (not yet married and then named Marie Grosholtz) and her mother were suspected of being royal sympathizers and so were imprisoned in the infamous La Force Prison. Once she was freed, Marie needed to prove her loyalty to the revolutionaries, which she did by making death masks of Louis XVI, Marie Antoinette, and other executed nobles. These skills would later come in handy and were the first step in what became a less gruesome worldwide attraction.

the stage of the Grand Ole Opry, record an album in a studio, and design a t-shirt for the merch booth on your world tour. There's music playing at every turn, so the experience is an immersive one, more than just a series of photo ops. But you'll still want to take a selfie with stars like Katy Perry.

In total, there are more than 50 wax figures, the majority of which were made specifically for the Nashville location. The likenesses of Taylor Swift, Billie Holiday, Bob Dylan, and country stars galore have been preserved for the ages. They may not be real, but this place is real fun.

Connect with...

5 Pedal the Music City Bikeway
30 Get deep into country music at the Hall of Fame

21 Play with your food at family-friendly restaurants

Families and Kids • Food

Why Go: Lots of restaurants have kid-friendly menus, dishes that appeal to those who want smaller portions of familiar favorites. But, true to form, Nashville's family-friendly eateries offer a little extra.

Where: There are spots on this list on the south, east, and west sides of town, as well as in Midtown, so location doesn't have to be a determining factor in where to have family fun.

Timing: Many of these spots have certain hours of the day (often early evening) when kids are welcome; later on, they morph into adults-only gathering places.

The **Pfunky Griddle** (2800 Bradford Ave., 615/298-2088, www.thepfunkygriddle.com) is perhaps the city's most popular kid-friendly eatery. Here, the tables are outfitted with hibachi-type grills. You order dishes like pancakes, eggs, or breakfast potatoes, and you're served the ingredients to cook on your own. Kids love choosing mix-ins to cook into their pancake batter—there are more than 20 options, including M&Ms, blueberries, and peanut butter. The menu includes many gluten-free options.

Drag queen brunch might not be on the obvious list to take the kids on the weekends, but the **Drag'n Brunch** at **Suzy Wong's House of Yum** (1515 Church St., 615/329-2913, www.suzywongsnashville.com) should change that. Suzy Wong is the alter ego of owner and *Top Chef* alumnus Arnold Myint, whose restaurant offers a riotous menu of Asian fusion shared plates. The weekend brunch features drag performers who interact with diners, spinning, winking, and dancing campily from table to table. The food is fun—think Asian nachos—rather than the traditional brunch dishes. There are plenty of vegetarian and gluten-free options on the menu, too.

The Pharmacy Burger Beer Garden (731 McFerrin Ave., 615/712-9517, http://thepharmacyburger.com) is a popular East Nashville beer garden and burger joint. In addition to the in-depth beer, bratwurst, and burger menu, the team at The Pharmacy makes their sodas

▲ Game Terminal

▲ Lockeland Table

▲ live music at Robert's Western World

by hand: The Creamsicle soda tastes just like that orange summertime treat. The kids' menu has all the typical options—chicken fingers and hot dogs—but the regular menu is so big that adventurous young eaters will find things they love. And that's even before they see the milkshake list. The big grassy backyard and beer garden make it a fun place to bring the kids. Waits can be long on warm weekends, but there's room for the kids to play.

Lockeland Table (1520 Woodland St., 615/228-4864, www.lockelandtable.com) is one of several small farm-to-fork restaurants in Nashville. While its cozy dining room and refined menu may not seem like a haven for kids, its daily Community Hour is designed for families. Order from the discounted Community Hour menu, which includes kid-pleasing options like grilled cheese sandwiches, pizzas, and apple slices with peanut butter, as well as tacos, *queso fundido* (similar to fondue), and seasonal dishes both adults and kids will crave. A portion of proceeds go to local schools.

Bring the family to **Game Terminal** (201 Terminal Ct., 615/610-2460, www.gameterminal.com) to play pinball games in a massive venue. Most games are priced at $0.50-1, but several rows of classic games, like *Pac-Man,* are free. Game options run the gamut from old-school pinball to interactive types that you navigate with a steering wheel, as well as table tennis and giant Jenga. Game Terminal hosts a rotating selection of food trucks; servers bring your food to you, so you can focus on the games, rather than standing in line. The venue is 21 and over after 8pm.

Head to **Bongo East/Game Point** (107 S. 11st St., 615/777-3278, https://gamepointcafe.com), a welcoming, casual café that has a library of more than 300 board games you can play while eating sandwiches, salads, and snacks. Games are categorized by type, age range, and length of play. An on-site concierge will help you find something that fits your interests.

The OneC1ty complex in Midtown is home to Gerald Craft's **Pastaria Nashville** (8 City Blvd., 615/915-1866, http://eatpastaria.com), a friendly Italian eatery with delicious wood-fired pizzas, fresh pastas, and amazing gelato. Kids are given butcher paper on which they can draw and create while they wait for their food. The outdoor area at OneC1ty has fun sculptures and open space where kids can run around, plus a sand volleyball court. It's an easy walk from Centennial Park and the Parthenon.

El Paseo Mexican Kitchen and Patio (905 51st Ave. N., 615/866-9517, www.elpaseonashville.com) was Nashville's first restaurant with its own dog park. This is where to bring the entire family, including Fido. Pups can play in the adjacent dog park, which you can see from the dog-friendly patio. Let the kids and pups romp at this eatery in The Nations while you feast on from-scratch tacos, salads, Mexican street corn, and a Mexican mac and cheese topped with crushed Doritos. There are even tacos for the dogs.

Many honky-tonks allow kids before 6pm, so tell 'em to grab a cowboy hat and get ready to kick up their heels. **Robert's Western World** (416B Broadway, 615/244-9552, http://robertswesternworld.com) has two great deals for budget-conscious families who want to experience the pleasure of a honky-tonk. The Recession Special is a fried bologna sandwich, chips, a Moon Pie, and a PBR for just $6. The Doggone Stimulus Package swaps in a beef corn dog and a Busch Light for $6.50. (The kid-friendly version subs a soda in for the beer.) Just don't forget to tip the band. The earlier in the day you go during the week, the better for families with children, as it will be quieter and less crowded.

Connect with...

🔟 Widen your perspective at historic Fort Negley

㉜ Explore kid-friendly museums

22 Get the best views of the city
from the John Seigenthaler Pedestrian Bridge

Be a Tourist in Your City

Why Go: There's nothing like a vantage point that allows you to experience the city not just as a concrete jungle, but as one surrounded by lush Tennessee greenery, a rolling river, and flowering cherry trees.

Where: John Seigenthaler Pedestrian Bridge, from Symphony Pl. and 3rd Ave. S. to S. 1st St. below Victory Ave. • Enter on either side by elevator, stairs, or a long ramp.

Timing: I recommend being on the bridge at sunset. You'll watch the sun lower behind downtown as Broadway's neon lights flicker on and the sky changes color.

The second Saturday in September has two great bridge-centric events. At the **Cumberland River Dragon Boat Festival** (www.dragonboatnashville.com), the bridge is a great vantage point from which to see the 40-foot boats race during the day. In the evening, during **Wine on the River** (www.wineontherivernashville.com), you can sip vino while surrounded by stunning city vistas.

Built in 1907, the John Seigenthaler Pedestrian Bridge spans the Cumberland River, connecting East Nashville to downtown. It was originally intended for vehicular traffic, but in 1998, the structure was converted to a pedestrian bridge. Today, the bridge functions as a convenient hub, as well as one of the best spots in the city for views.

Walking across the bridge has become my favorite way to travel into downtown. As I walk underneath the geometric trusses and cross the Cumberland River, I take in the city views and absorb the energy of all the other people on the bridge. If there's a hockey game, people will be wearing gold Predators jerseys; if there's a big show at the Ryman, there'll be plenty of sequins and cowboy boots.

I always make a point to stop in the middle to check out the skyline with the Batman building looming large. The partiers on the pedal taverns cheer and laugh, and the live music floats up to me as the neon flashes in time on Broadway. The barges slowly make their way up and down the Cumberland River. For the best views, step onto one of the platforms that jut out from the bridge.

▲ the bridge at night

John Seigenthaler Pedestrian Bridge

▲ view of the Batman building from the bridge

▲ people walking across the bridge

The bridge also serves as the anchor for several of the city's greenways. On the west end of the pedestrian bridge, you can connect with the Greenway at Riverfront Park. Circle Ascend Amphitheatre and watch the Music City Star train lumber by. Farther north, the Cumberland River Greenway continues to First Horizon Park, the city's minor league baseball stadium. To the east of the bridge is the East Bank Greenway. Head north and you'll get good views of the bridge plus the red *Ghost Ballet* sculpture. While its giant, curved metal pieces may look like old track from a roller coaster, don't let any old-timers pull your leg: It's a piece of abstract art, not remnants from Opryland. You'll then cruise right past Nissan Stadium, where the Tennessee Titans play. If you head south on the greenway, you'll end up in the small Cumberland Park, home to native, pollinator-friendly plants, climbing walls for kids, and a splash pad perfect for cooling off on a hot summer day.

In its history, it has also been called the Sparkman Street Bridge and the Shelby Street Pedestrian Bridge. Today, most folks just call it the pedestrian bridge. No matter what it's called, though, I love getting to walk over it twice a day. By the time I'm ready to head back to East

In the Spotlight

For a period of time, when the show *Nashville* was the nighttime soap opera that everyone was watching, the pedestrian bridge seemed like the most photographed spot in town. If the show's characters had a dramatic discussion, a secret to share, or an illicit tryst, they were shown here. In real life, it's a popular spot, and not where to go if you don't want to be seen or overheard.

Nashville, the sun has long set and the stars are out. The bridge's bright white steel lights up against the dark sky. While other people wait in their cars to exit parking garages, I get a peaceful stroll, appreciating the city as it settles down for the night. With the bridge almost to myself, I stop to look at its reflection in the water below. Beyond, to the south, is the colorful lit-up arch of the Korean Veterans Memorial Bridge, also reflected in the river. It's the perfect ending to a night downtown.

Connect with...

5 Pedal the Music City Bikeway

12 Go backstage at the Ryman Auditorium

23 Toast the legacy of Printers Alley

Be a Tourist in Your City • Neighborhoods and City Streets

Why Go: Printers Alley is more than just a concentration of nightlife hot spots: This historic district has a long and storied past—and much of it centers on alcohol in ways you might not expect.

Where: Downtown • from Union St. to Church St., between 3rd Ave. N. and 4th Ave. N. • http://printersalley.com

Note: Though the addresses of some of the alley's venues are on a main street (often connected to a hotel), they will open out onto the alley with a separate entrance.

Timing: Printers Alley wakes up at night. If you're not up for crowds of revelers and tourists who've had a beer or three, come earlier in the evening. If you want to attend a burlesque performance, plan to come later.

Founded in 1828, Printers Alley is named after Nashville's storied printing industry. For almost a century, this small alley has been a bustling center of activity—some legal, some not, some you might not want to write home about. In the early 1900s, this area was home to two newspapers (*The Tennessean,* which is still the city's daily, and the *Nashville Banner*), plus more than a dozen other publishers and 10 print shops. As late as the 1960s, there were still 36 printers in the area. The last printer moved out of the alley in the 1970s, but the name remains.

In the early 1900s, men who worked for the printers would congregate in the alley after they punched out for the day, and it became known as the Men's Quarter. Liquor manufacturing in the state was illegal even before Prohibition, but from 1909 to 1939, plenty of people spent their time in the alley's speakeasies having a drink, bringing their own liquor to these secret bars in unmarked brown bags. Even after Prohibition ended, it still wasn't legal to buy alcohol by the drink, so this practice of brown-bagging continued in Printers Alley. The area's illicit reputation was furthered by the opening of a brothel and a casino during this period.

During the 1940s, nightclubs opened in the alley; over the years, performers including Dottie West, Chet Atkins, Waylon Jennings, The Supremes, and even Jimi Hendrix graced

Printers Alley

these stages. From 1948 to 1998, a man named David "Skull" Schulman ran one of these clubs, called Skull's Rainbow Room, featuring burlesque dancers with a live band accompaniment. Folks called him "the mayor of Printers Alley" for his longevity and commitment to the community. He was a character; after appearing on the campy country music variety show *Hee Haw,* he would wear his TV overalls at the bar. He even dyed the fur of his poodles, Sweetie and Sugar, red and green at Christmas. In 1998, when he was 80, Schulman was setting up his bar for the night when he was robbed and murdered. The city mourned his loss, and for many years Printers Alley languished. People even said the spot was haunted.

Over the years, development came with an eye toward restoration. Now a nationally recognized historic district, Printers Alley impresses lovers of architecture with its original brick buildings and preserved ornate iron balconies. The pedestrian-only street maintains its clandestine feel with funky neon signage, crowded storefronts with metal doors, and towering brick facades that feel more like the French Quarter in New Orleans than the typical wide blocks of Nashville's downtown.

entrance to Printers Alley

A beautiful arched neon sign with a silhouette of a printer marks the entrance to Printers Alley. It's one of Nashville's most photographed objects. It lights up at night, but even during the day it's worth seeing. Stand in the middle of Church Street and you can see how it frames Nissan Stadium across the river.

Printers Alley and adjacent Bankers Alley are thriving today, thanks to the area's popularity with tourists. But locals, too, will have a lot of fun visiting this unique entertainment strip. The biggest name, of course, is **Skull's Rainbow Room** (222 Printers Alley, 615/810-9631, www.skullsrainbowroom.com), which was lovingly brought back by Bill and Shannon Miller (the folks behind Nudie's Honky Tonk and the Johnny Cash and Patsy Cline Museums). Skull's still offers burlesque performances by feather-clad professional dancers, along with live jazz seven days a week.

Other bars and restaurants have embraced the alley's playfully illicit vibes, with hidden entrances, dark interiors, and well-crafted cocktails. If you want food and drink that encompass the speakeasy attitude, check out **Black Rabbit** (218 3rd Ave. N., 615/891-2380) and **Jane's Hideaway** (209 3rd Ave. N., 615/942-7809, www.janeshideaway.com). Some of these spots, like **Snitch** (206 Printers Alley, 615/622-1491) and **Bobby's Garage Bar** (230 4th Ave. N., 615/782-7100) are connected to boutique hotels (Dream Nashville and the Bobby, respectively), which offer a way to experience the history and the vibrancy of the alley from different vantage points.

Sure, Printers Alley might feel a little cheesy at first glance, but when you dig a little deeper, you'll find more substance. It's a place to connect to the past and enjoy some of the city's longtime indulgences—legal ones, of course.

Connect with...

7 Kick up your heels at a honky-tonk
17 Hear up-and-coming musicians first
40 Sip your way down the Tennessee Whiskey Trail

24 Strum and pick your way through local guitar shops

Why Go: This is Music City. The boots and the rhinestone-bedecked jackets are just accessories. To really fit in, what you need is six strings and something to say.

Where: Citywide, with a concentration near The Gulch and in East Nashville

Timing: It's always possible you'll run into a celebrity when you head to a guitar shop in Nashville, but the odds increase during Tin Pan South in March or the Americana Music Festival in September. Lots of musicians keep "rock 'n' roll hours," so music shops may be quieter first thing in the morning.

When I first moved to Nashville, I thought it was a joke when people said there were more guitars than people in the city. But I quickly found out that even the most casual musicians have multiple guitars. It's not unusual for a performer to have one guitar they use for songwriting, one for shows, an acoustic, and an electric. Around here, the formula for how many guitars you need is X+1, with X being the number you currently have. That means there's always a reason to go guitar shopping.

Nashville specializes in small guitar shops with big selections, lots of handmade and customizable instruments, and quality used gear. At many shops, you can even have vintage musical instruments restored. When you're ready to start browsing, have a budget and an idea of what you need in advance—like car shopping, it doesn't make sense to test drive a luxury model if you need something more affordable. Whether you're ready to buy or you just want to dream, you can spend a day perusing these Music City staples:

Since 1928, four generations of family members at **Delgado Guitars** (919 Gallatin Ave., 615/227-4578, http://delgadoguitars.com) have specialized in classic guitars, square-necks, ukuleles, and bass guitars, made by hand for generations. From their shop in East Nashville, the Delgados, who pass along their craft to each new generation of the family, can also repair and restore older instruments.

Gruhn Guitars (2120 8th Ave. S., 615/256-2033, http://guitars.com) has been a fixture in

1: Corner Music **2:** Delgado Guitars **3:** Fanny's House of Music **4:** Carter Vintage Guitars

Nashville since 1970, first in tiny digs downtown, and now in an expansive space on 8th Avenue South that has room for more than 1,100 instruments. You can't possibly choose an instrument without knowing how it sounds, so at Gruhn, as at most shops in town, you are encouraged to take the guitars off their racks and play them.

It's not unusual at **Fanny's House of Music** (1101 Holly St., 615/750-5746, www.fannyshouseofmusic.com) to have test sessions turn into jam sessions with other musicians who are hanging around this popular East Nashville gathering place. Fanny's sells both vintage and used instruments, and because the business is owned by women, it specializes in instruments that are sized for female performers; these are often smaller and lighter than the standard options. It's not just guitars here, but drums and amps, too, plus groovy vintage clothing to complete your stage look.

Compared to Delgado and Gruhn, **Carter Vintage Guitars** (625 8th Ave. S., 615/915-1851, http://cartervintage.com) seems like a relative newcomer—it didn't open until 2012—but the owners are anything but inexperienced. Christy and Walter Carter each have more than

▲ specialty guitars at Corner Music

a quarter-century of background playing guitars and can help you find the right one. Carter Vintage Guitars also has a deep inventory of celebrity-owned instruments, if you want to take home an instrument that has seen the bright lights of the stage. If you want to strum the same guitar Steve Earle played, this is the place to go. You'll know you are in the right place when you see the mural on the north side of the building, featuring multiple guitars.

Corner Music (3048 Dickerson Pike, 615/297-9559, http://cornermusic.com) has its own YouTube channel, so you can hear what folks play on their gear. They price match big-box stores for many of the instruments they sell.

From the Track One building in Wedgewood-Houston, **Artisan Guitars** (1201 4th Ave. S., 615/595-2544, http://artisanguitars.com) makes custom acoustic guitars. The showroom is open to the public, but by appointment, so call first. Once you're there, you can have them make you an instrument that's worthy of being a family heirloom. You can even do a trade-in of your current guitar to help pay for the upgrade.

Near the Grand Ole Opry, **Blues Vintage Guitars** (212 McGavock Pike, 615/613-1389, www.bluesvintageguitars.com) is best known for their used guitars. They also do repair work and set ups of pre-owned instruments. You may have less elbow room in the small showroom, but there are still plenty of instruments from which to choose. They also carry new instruments, including banjos, keyboards, and saxophones.

Marty Lanham, a former repairman at Gruhn Guitars, creates custom-made guitars for your particular style and sound at **Nashville Guitar Company** (615/557-4394, http://nashvilleguitarcompany.com). Call for an appointment and you'll be given the shop's Inglewood address. Once there you'll have an intimate experience where you can decide on the size, wood, grip, and custom inlays of your guitar to-be. Lanham also restores vintage instruments and offers set ups.

Connect with...
❶ Try your hand at songwriting
⓱ Hear up-and-coming musicians first
㉖ Rhapsodize about your favorites at music museums

25 Feed your mind in North Nashville

Neighborhoods and City Streets • Black Heritage • Food

Why Go: Wandering through two historic neighborhoods in North Nashville will leave both your mind and your belly full.

Where: Germantown and Salemtown are a mile north of downtown and just north of the Tennessee State Capitol building and Jefferson Street • www.historicgermantown. org

Timing: It takes less than an hour to walk leisurely from the capitol to the north end of Salemtown. Daytime is best for exploring these areas on foot.

Germantown and Salemtown are dotted with cozy architecture and stately churches, surrounded by leafy streets, and rich with restaurants and shops. Both are rooted in history; Germantown was built in the 1850s by European immigrants. Once working-class neighborhoods, they are more gentrified. Germantown has more restaurants, breweries, and yoga studios—and more tourists—than quieter Salemtown.

▲ Big Al's Deli

North of downtown, Germantown runs from Jefferson Street to Hume Street between the Cumberland River and the interstate. Above Hume Street is tiny Salemtown, occupying about 12 blocks in its entirety.

Start your walk at the **Bicentennial Capitol Mall State Park** (600 James Robertson Pkwy., 615/741-5280, http://tnstateparks.com), which honors the state's first 200 years. Study up on Tennessee's past by checking out the history lessons inscribed in stone along the west end of the park. Follow the inscriptions to the north end, where 95 carillon bells (for the state's 95 counties) play "The Tennessee Waltz," "Rocky Top," and other Tennessee-themed songs on the hour. On the east side of the park is a re-creation of the state's topography in plants, featuring species from the bluffs of the Mississippi River to the Great Smoky Mountains.

Barista Parlor

scoreboard at First Horizon Park

Steamboys

Silver Sands Café

Head north to **First Horizon Park** (19 Junior Gilliam Way, 615/690-4487, https://first-horizonpark.com), the home of MLB's minor league Nashville Sounds. The stadium was built in 2015 on the site of **Sulphur Dell,** which was Nashville's baseball stadium from 1885 to 1963. In the latter half of the 1940s, this was where the Nashville Cubs, a Negro League team, played their games. As you walk by, admire the guitar-shaped scoreboard. The best views are from 3rd Avenue North.

Cross Jefferson Street to reach Germantown's narrow streets, lined with stylish homes and cozy carriage houses. Before continuing further, you might want a bite to eat. Luckily, this area has lots of restaurants. West of the Bicentennial Mall is **Silver Sands Café** (937 Locklayer St., 615/780-9900, www.silversandsnashville.com), a family-owned meat-and-three cafeteria beloved by chefs across the city. For a light meal of dumplings and *bao,* head toward the Cumberland River to **Steamboys** (1200 2nd Ave. N., 615/678-6336, www.steamboys.com), which was dreamt up by five friends with a common love of Chinese comfort food. For something lighter, grab a sweet snack at **The Christie Cookie Co.** (1205 3rd Ave. N., 615/242-3817, www.christiecookies.com) or a cup of coffee at **Barista Parlor** (1230 4th Ave. N., 615/401-9144, http://baristaparlor.com).

On the west side of Germantown, check out the **Werthan Mills building** (1400 Rosa L. Parks Blvd.). In 1871, this mammoth brick textile factory employed many of the people who lived in the neighborhood. The main mill building is now an apartment complex called **Werthan Lofts.** Its exterior maintains the same commanding presence it had more than a century ago.

Morgan Recreation Center (411 Hume St.) was turned into a park for those who worked in the neighborhood's textile mills in 1909. Today, it has green space, a playground, and a replica of the sulfur spring that attracted folks here in the 1800s, looking for a "fountain of youth."

As you move from Germantown into Salemtown, you'll see yellow street signs along Hume Street marking the transition. Hume Street, the delineation between the neighborhoods, is where you'll find **Fehr School** (1624 Rep. John Lewis Way N.), one of the first desegregated schools in Nashville. In 1957 it was the site of protests by more than 400 angry white segregationists who marched from the state capitol to try to intimidate Black families and prevent

Come Back Soon

Return to Germantown and Salemtown in the evening for dinner and drinks at some of the area's exciting restaurants.

Henrietta Red (1200 4th Ave. N., 615/490-8042, www.henriettared.com) is an oyster bar with marble-topped counters and impeccable service.

The acclaimed **City House** (1222 4th Ave. N., 615/76-5838, http://cityhousenashville.com) serves modern Italian cuisine with a twist.

Rolf and Daughters (700 Taylor St., 615/866-9897, www.rolfanddaughters.com), downstairs in the Werthan Lofts, is praised for its pasta and has a lovely patio.

Butchertown Hall (1416 4th Ave. N., 615/454-3634, www.butchertownhall.com) is a buzzy space with smoky brisket, tacos, and cocktails.

them from enrolling their children in the elementary school. You can't go inside the original two-story brick building, but a sign by the door notes its history.

You may be ready for a hearty meal as you approach the north end of Salemtown. Head to **Big Al's Deli** (1827 4th Ave. N., 615/242-8118, www.bigalsdeliandcatering.com), a meat-and-three-style restaurant with a rotating menu. The jerk chicken and smashed potatoes are highlights, but the real draw is meeting Al and hearing his stories. After your meal you can head back south; take different streets to admire more of the area.

Connect with...

6 Celebrate Black culture and history on Jefferson Street

35 Wander the Buchanan Arts District

26 Rhapsodize about your favorites at music museums

Only in Nashville • Art and Culture

Why Go: Take a deep dive into some of the tallest tales of your favorite music, artists, and venues.

Where: The majority of these museums are in the heart of downtown or just a few blocks away. Tickets to each of these museums can top $20. If you plan to visit all of them, the **Music City Total Access Pass** (www.visitmusiccity.com, $99) is worth considering.

Timing: While these museums are chock-full of artifacts and memorabilia, none of them have giant collections. You can visit a few in a day without suffering from information overload.

People say that the thing that makes Nashville different from other music-centric cities is that here, it's all about the song. Songs can tell stories that are personal and also universal. So where better to immerse yourself in those stories than at a music museum?

In January 2021, the **National Museum of African American Music** (510 Broadway, 615/301-8724, http://nmaam.org) opened its doors to show the world its comprehensive collection of Black music spanning more than 50 genres. Start in the 190-seat Roots Theater, where you'll watch a film about the origins of Black music. Continue into artifact-filled, interactive rooms, which walk you through Mississippi Delta blues, hip-hop, gospel, and more. You'll take audio quizzes, create your own tunes, and compete in a rap battle. By the end of your journey, you'll have learned about the Harlem Renaissance, danced with *Soul Train,* and teared up with a crowd watching Prince's 2007 Super Bowl halftime performance on an oversized screen. You can spend many hours here if you want to see and hear every detail, but you can also breeze through in an hour and still have a great time.

Known as "the Possum," George Jones was a country music great, famous for his storytelling ballads. He passed away in 2013 at the age of 81, and his remarkable musical legacy is detailed at the riverfront **George Jones Museum** (128 2nd Ave. N., 615/818-0128, http://

Johnny Cash Museum

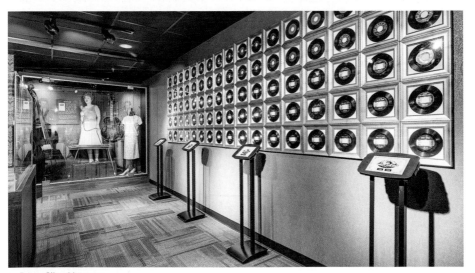

Patsy Cline Museum

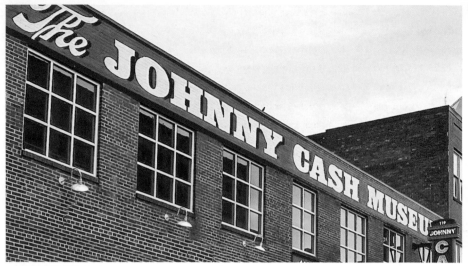

Johnny Cash Museum

georgejones.com/museum). Filled with artifacts from his life and career, from stage costumes and color-coordinated guitars to awards, the museum celebrates his accomplishments but also tells of his tribulations. Jones struggled with alcohol abuse: He famously once drove a John Deere tractor to the liquor store because his brother-in-law hid his car keys. And, yes, a replica of that John Deere tractor is front and center in the museum. Some exhibits include a hologram of Jones, to give the experience of seeing the legend live and in person.

The **Johnny Cash Museum** (119 3rd Ave. S., 615/256-1777, www.johnnycashmuseum. com) is a cornerstone of country music history in downtown Nashville. The museum's collection was amassed by one fan-turned-collector and features interactive listening booths, the jumpsuit that the Man in Black wore when he flipped the bird in public, and other memorabilia from his varied and lauded career. Locals are especially fond of the rebuilt stone wall that was taken from Cash's suburban Nashville home.

Housed above the Johnny Cash Museum, the **Patsy Cline Museum** (119 3rd Ave. S., 615/454-4722, www.patsymuseum.com) might seem like an afterthought from the outside. But once you get inside, you'll see it's anything but. The museum offers small but poignant displays about the life of legendary country artist Patsy Cline, who died in a plane crash in 1963 at the age of 30. Cline, known best for her song "Crazy," was one of the first country artists to cross over to mainstream charts. Many of her personal belongings, such as a wedding photo album, were donated by her family. Exhibits include a replica of the soda shop where Cline worked and one of her home, complete with a living room arranged around a phonograph. There are also multiple videos covering her career. Admission is separate from the Johnny Cash Museum.

The Rhinestone Cowboy was known as one of music's best guitar players. The **Glen Campbell Museum** (111 Broadway, 615/258-5576, www.glencampbellmuseum.com) tells his rags-to-riches story, noting his considerable contributions to pop and country music and, later in life, gospel music. Campbell even played with The Beach Boys in 1964 and 1965 and was a session musician with The Monkees. But he's best known and beloved for his songs, including "Southern Nights," "Gentle on My Mind," and the tearjerker "Wichita Lineman." The museum has many of the stringed instruments Campbell played on display. You'll also find costumes (many with rhinestones, naturally), and a set from his *Goodtime Hour* TV variety show, which ran from 1969 to 1972.

Not to be confused with the Country Music Hall of Fame, the **Musicians Hall of Fame & Museum** (401 Gay St., 615/244-3263, www.musicianshalloffame.com) honors the people, regardless of genre, who make the songs that we tap our toes to: the session musicians, the sound engineers, and the producers who you may never have heard of. The MHOF displays guitars from Jimi Hendrix and Glen Campbell, but even more fascinating are the memorabilia and instruments from the unsung heroes of the industry. Learn about session musicians, who play for multiple stars, and how genres from the Muscle Shoals sound to Motown are linked. The interactive Grammy Museum Gallery on the first floor walks you through the process of writing and recording a hit. The exhibits throughout are dense, with lots of elements to read and listen to.

Connect with...

12 Go backstage at the Ryman Auditorium
30 Get deep into country music at the Hall of Fame

27 Feast on Kurdish food

Little Kurdistan

Food • Neighborhoods and City Streets

Why Go: As the city with the largest Kurdish population in the United States, Nashville offers an opportunity to better understand—and taste—Kurdish culture.

Where: Little Kurdistan, 7 miles south of downtown • Nolensville Pike and Elysian Fields Ct. • It's useful to have a car to get here if you're coming from downtown.

Timing: Go when you're hungry. The best way to experience the community as a first-timer is to come for lunch or dinner.

Nashville has a population of about 15,000 Kurdish American residents, more than any other city in the United States. Many of these people came to Nashville as refugees beginning in the late 1970s, fleeing political upheavals, genocide, and the dictatorship of Saddam Hussein. They hail from the Kurdish region of the Middle East, which overlaps the borders of Iran, Iraq, Syria, and Turkey; the Kurds are the largest ethnic group in the world without their own fully autonomous land. While the first wave of Kurdish refugees in Nashville numbered just 50, over the next several decades the population grew. Today, some of the refugees and immigrants refer to themselves as "Amerikurds," a portmanteau of "American" and "Kurd."

While Kurdish people live all over the Nashville area, the community known as Little Kurdistan is concentrated in South Nashville, on Nolensville Pike. If you're envisioning Chinatown in San Francisco or Little Italy in New York, it's worth adjusting your expectations. Little Kurdistan is a small area dotted with shops and restaurants, many of which are nestled into strip malls off busy Nolensville Pike.

The best way for a newcomer to experience Nashville's Kurdish culture is by eating, whether by sitting down at a restaurant, grabbing takeout, or shopping the markets and trying recipes at home. Kurdish food often includes flatbreads and kabobs, with lots of lamb and chicken, plus rice dishes. Many Kurds are Muslim and do not drink alcohol, so black tea is a more common beverage than beer.

inside Edessa Restaurant

Edessa Restaurant

129

While many of Nashville's Kurdish eateries are casual spots, **Edessa Restaurant** (3802 Nolensville Pike, 615/837-2567, www.edessanashville.com) offers a more upscale dining experience. Cozy booths and attentive service accompany the Turkish dishes of beef and lamb, lentil and bean soups, and salads. The appetizers feature some Turkish delicacies, as well as dishes that may be familiar to fans of Middle Eastern food, like falafel and tabbouleh. The owners of Edessa also have a restaurant in downtown's Assembly Food Hall.

Named for the celebration of spring that many Kurds observe, **Newroz Market** (393 Elysian Fields Ct., 615/333-0037) is a go-to shop for black tea, baklava, halal meats, and groceries. You'll see locals heading straight to the back, to **House of Shawarma,** a sandwich counter with a small seating area inside the market. The chicken sandwich is a popular pick.

The shawarma, wrapped in fresh-baked bread, is the popular to-go item at **Sulav International Market** (4647 Nolensville Pike, 615/915-2557), which also stocks favorite imported ingredients and sells produce and halal meats.

Seven days a week, **Azadi International Food Market and Bakery** (391 Elysian

▲ Little Kurdistan

Community Focus

Established in 1998, the **Salahadeen Center of Nashville** (364 Elysian Fields Ct., 615/333-0530, www.scntn.org) was the first Kurdish mosque to operate in North America. This community center is now a focal point of Muslim life in Nashville, offering language classes and kids' programming (even a soccer league), as well as worship.

Fields Ct., 615/315-0904) provides the community with fresh-baked bread pulled from the brick oven behind the shop. You can grab meat- or cheese-topped breads, *sambusa* (a samosa-like snack), or shawarma. The grocery has a popular halal butcher counter, too. The bread is baked all day, so there's no rush to be there when the doors open.

Closer to downtown, **Istanbul** (2631 Nolensville Pike, 615/248-6888) has been serving Turkish foods in Nashville for more than two decades. Owner Memet Arslan uses recipes that he brought to the United States from the café he owned in Turkey. The dishes served blend both Turkish and Kurdish traditions. In addition to dips, vegetarian dishes, and kabobs, there are also American classics like burgers. The owners of Istanbul also have a restaurant in the Assembly Food Hall downtown. Nearby on Thompson Lane, **House of Kabob** (407 W. Thompson Ln., 615/333-3711) serves a fusion of Persian and Kurdish foods, including *kubideh* (ground beef kebab), gyros, and other meats on a stick.

Connect with...

36 Taste the international flavors of Nolensville Pike

28 Treat yourself to custom-made boots

Shopping • Only in Nashville

Why Go: Boots are the ultimate fashion equalizer in Nashville, worn by bachelorettes on pedal taverns, university professors in lecture halls, and stars walking the red carpet. When you're ready to commit, nothing tops a bespoke pair.

Where: 12South and suburban Brentwood are home to the area's best bootmakers.

Timing: Custom leathercraft doesn't happen overnight. It takes more than 30 hours to make a pair of handcrafted boots. Plus, there's often demand, so expect to wait weeks or months for your new pair.

Question: Which of the following happened to me?

1. I met country singer Toby Keith at a press event, and he said, "I tried to talk to you earlier when I saw you in the lobby because I wanted to ask you about your boots."

2. After I interviewed a local computer scientist for a magazine article, he emailed me and asked for the best places in town to buy his daughter boots.

3. A street busker stopped me on Broadway as I walked by and told the assembled tourists that I must be a local because of my boots.

▲ Music City Leather

Answer: All of the above. And each was about a different pair of boots. (I actually stopped wearing the pair with Ukrainian embroidery that Toby Keith noticed when I run errands, because too many people want to chat about them.) Good cowboy boots are expensive, but they can last a lifetime if you take care of them. If you can afford it, the investment in a custom-made pair, just as you want them, is one that will more than pay off over time. Work with a bootmaker to choose your favorite colors and cuts, a pointed toe or a squared-off one, a low heel or a high one. Good boots should fit like a good handshake: firm enough to hold on, but not so much that they cause discomfort. Boots may be a little tight at first but will adjust as the leather softens.

Chief in the game is Wes Shugart of **Music City Leather** (Brentwood, 615/533-4882, www.musiccityleather.com). While there isn't a public shop to browse, if you make an appointment, you can have Shugart handcraft the boots of your dreams: ones that are comfortable enough to be worn and spiffy enough to turn heads. If you don't already know what you want, Shugart will help with the creative process, showing you past creations and options for leather type and color. He then takes eight different measurements of your foot and molds the leather, resulting in a pair of boots that's perfectly suited to you. The whole process takes about a year and costs $2,000-5,000. It's an investment, but you can expect to have these boots for a lifetime.

Jaylin Ramer relocated her successful boot shop, **Planet Cowboy** (2905 12th Ave. S., 615/730-5789, http://planetcowboy.com) from New York to Nashville in 2020, giving locals another option for quality, one-of-a-kind boots. About one-third of Planet Cowboy's stock is custom-designed by Ramer. While it's possible to browse the cozy shop whenever it's open, it's best to make an appointment if you want custom boots, so you can go through the process with minimal distractions. Ramer's outgoing personality comes through in her designs, which include lots of bright colors. After the design is set, the boots are made in a factory. Prices start around $900 and the process takes 2-5 months. The store also stocks boots by Rios of Mercedes and Stallion.

If you want a little bit of personalization, rather than a full custom fit and design, try **Lucchese Bootmaker** (503 12th Ave. S., 615/242-1161, www.lucchese.com), a Texas brand with Italian roots in The Gulch. Browse this sleek, brick-front shop with its high ceilings and meticulously arranged pairs of leather boots, which start at $1,700. Note the elements you like, and then personalize your own pair: You'll pick the silhouette, heel, toe shape, and decorative elements, then the boots are made in a factory.

Connect with...

14 Learn to two-step or line dance
24 Strum and pick your way through local guitar shops

29 Bask in the beauty of Belle Meade Boulevard

Scenic Drives • Neighborhoods and City Streets

Why Go: Belle Meade Boulevard is a short but lovely scenic drive, perfect for a respite from the bustle of city life.

Where: Between Harding Pike and Warner Park, about 6 miles west of downtown

Timing: Go on a beautiful summer day, when it's warm enough to appreciate your car's air-conditioning, but still cool enough that you'll have fun outside. In spring, enjoy the bursts of color when the cherry, redbud, and dogwood trees are in bloom. You won't need much time to do the drive, but it's easy to spend a full morning or afternoon at Cheekwood or the park.

Normally when you think of going for a scenic drive, you're envisioning yourself out in the country, perhaps with a picnic in the trunk. But Belle Meade Boulevard is a short jaunt just outside the city that takes you through landscaped opulence, by outdoor sculptures and architectural gems, ending at a park and a pastoral 1930s estate that's open to the public.

This three-mile stretch of roadway was originally created in 1913, as a way to connect the growing city of Nashville to new residential developments on the site of what had been the Belle Meade Plantation. Today, Belle Meade is a town of its own, sitting on the southwestern edge of Nashville. Pretty Belle Meade Boulevard winds past ornate homes, a synagogue, and private schools, ending at the Cheekwood estate and Warner Parks. It's the embodiment of well-heeled living, lined with seven- and eight-figure homes, blooming azaleas, and perfectly green lawns. The divided road has roomy lanes, each about 25 feet wide. In the middle is a landscaped median with sculptures scattered along it.

As you approach the boulevard, take a look at **St. George's Episcopal Church** (4715 Harding Pike), an elegant white-brick structure. The church had been planned since before the Depression, but construction didn't start until 1949.

Turn onto Belle Meade and you'll immediately spot **bronze sculptures** of a mare and foal by artist Gwen Reardon, the official animals of Belle Meade. (The former plantation was

mare and foal sculptures by artist Gwen Reardon on Belle Meade Boulevard

Cheekwood

also a renowned horse farm.) When Nashville's football and hockey teams are in the playoffs, the sculptures are decorated in Titans or Predators gear. But no other decorations are permitted, and once the playoffs are over, the uniforms must come down. Belle Meade is also marked by street signs that feature silhouettes of the mare and foal.

Next, you'll see **Immanuel Baptist Church** (222 Belle Meade Blvd.), a congregation that has existed since 1887. This brick-columned building, with its tall, white steeple, was built in 1954.

Between the cross streets of Tyne Boulevard and Forsythe Place, you'll see *Racoons and the Magic Horseshoes* by sculptor Nancy Schön. This installation features three life-sized bronze raccoons romping on the grass between two large horseshoes made from local stone. It's whimsical and lifelike, and a particular favorite of kids.

The end of the boulevard is marked by a series of restored Depression-era sandstone columns. This is the **Percy Warner Memorial Entrance** to the **Edwin and Percy Warner Parks** (1225 Belle Meade Blvd., www.warnerparks.org). An inscription at the entrance reads,

Percy Warner Memorial Entrance

Local Lore

Cheekwood owes its existence to the success of the coffee brand Maxwell House. During the 1920s, Leslie Cheek and Mabel Wood invested in the new coffee brand being developed by their cousin, Joel Cheek. Maxwell House proved to be a success and earned the Cheeks a fortune, which they used to buy the land that is now Cheekwood.

"So that future generations may continue to enjoy the beauty of wood and field and flower, this gateway to the park has been restored to its original splendor in memory of Percy Warner." Continue through the tree-lined, columned gate to find parking and the historic **Allée staircase** designed by Bryant Fleming, built in the 1930s. Take the staircase up into the 3,100-acre Warner Park (as locals call it). It includes hiking trails, a dog park, some of the only equestrian trails in the area, and a nature center with lots of family-friendly programming.

The other option is to turn right just before the park entrance and follow the signs to **Cheekwood** (200 Forrest Park Dr., 615/356-8000, http://cheekwood.org). In the late 1920s, Leslie Cheek and his wife, Mabel Wood, bought a large swath of land outside Nashville. They hired residential and landscape architect Bryant Fleming to create a 30,000-square-foot mansion and neighboring gardens. Cheekwood was completed in 1933 and opened to the public in 1960. Today, it houses a botanic garden, sculpture garden, and, in the original Georgian mansion, a small museum. Stroll through the green, wooded property and you may forget that you're near a major city. Walk the **Carell Woodland Sculpture Trail** to gaze at works by internationally acclaimed artists or wander past the water garden to the Japanese garden. There are dogwoods, an herb garden, delightful plantings of boxwoods, and much more. Galleries in the mansion contain American and European art, including excellent contemporary works. Cheekwood has the largest public collection of art by William Edmondson, a Nashville sculptor and stoneworker.

As you head back out on Belle Meade Boulevard, returning the way you came, you'll be surrounded once again by manicured greenery. It's clear how Belle Meade got its name, French for "beautiful meadow."

30 Get deep into country music
at the Country Music Hall of Fame and Museum

Only in Nashville • Be a Tourist in Your City

Why Go: No other place provides so much historical context about what made Nashville into Music City—plus it's just a good time, thanks to world-class exhibits, incredible music, and an engaging, immersive design.

Where: Country Music Hall of Fame and Museum, downtown, 222 Rep. John Lewis Way/5th Ave. S., 615/416-2001, http://countrymusichalloffame.org • 9am-5pm daily • admission $26 adults, $24 seniors and students, $16 children

Timing: Visit during the week when there isn't a major event in town, and you'll have all the time and privacy you want to listen at the museum's various interactive stations. Check the website for special events, such as live music performances.

When friends come to visit me in Nashville for the first time, I take them to the Country Music Hall of Fame and Museum, regardless of whether or not they think they're a country music fan. In fact, I'm *more* likely to take them if they claim not to be. The museum is a monument to country music, quite literally: Vertical windows at the front and back of the building resemble piano keys; from above, the museum resembles a bass clef. Inside, exhibits chart the genre's evolution, demonstrating that country music is so much more than what's currently playing on the radio.

Every time I've been (and I'm a member, so I've been a lot), I watch someone listen to an audio clip or examine memorabilia, and say something like, "I loved watching *The Kate Smith Show* growing up! I never think of *that* as country." Every time.

I, too, used to be someone who thought the museum represented just a single, narrow genre. Before I moved to Nashville in 2007, a friend brought me here. He stopped me at a video of Wanda Jackson, the Queen of Rockabilly, playing guitar, singing, and dancing in a fringed dress. The footage is decades old, so it's not the best technical sound. But it rings loud, full of talent, joy, and longevity: Jackson, born in 1937, didn't retire from performing until 2019. I hadn't considered how rockabilly and country were linked before that. It gave me a new per-

Country Music Hall of Fame and Museum

Hall of Fame rotunda

spective on country music, and it made me want to move to Nashville, where music is constantly evolving and where creativity is highly valued.

At the museum, which leads you on a one-way, chronological route through the history of country music and its myriad siblings, there are half a dozen private listening booths where you can hear studio-quality recordings and witness seminal, groundbreaking performances. See a few of the genre's most famous instruments: Bill Monroe's mandolin, Maybelle Carter's Gibson, and Hank Williams's Martin D-28. Other exhibits detail the rise of high-energy bluegrass, dance-friendly honky-tonk, and the smooth and sophisticated Nashville Sound, which introduced country music to new audiences. Temporary exhibits tend to have a more contemporary bent and focus on one artist, such as Emmylou Harris or Carrie Underwood.

You'll end your tour in the Hall of Fame, set in a high, solemn rotunda. Brass plaques honor the 100-plus inductees. High above the plaques, up toward the windows that allow a cathedral-like quality of light to filter through, are the words "Will the Circle Be Unbroken," from the hymn made famous by the Carter family.

Part of a visit to the museum includes a field trip of sorts. The only way to visit Music Row's famous **Historic RCA Studio B** (1611 Roy Acuff Pl., 615/416-2001, https://studiob.org, $20), where Elvis once recorded, is to buy a ticket at the museum box office (or from its website) and hop on a tour bus. At the studio, you get to hear the acoustics as they were when Elvis's voice filled the room. You'll have an opportunity to play a few keys on the piano and hear for yourself. The guided tour takes about an hour, including the 10-minute drive to Music Row and back. The tour is an additional fee to your admission and is worth the time and cost.

Downstairs, outside of the museum itself but in the same complex, is the landmark letterpress shop **Hatch Show Print** (224 Rep. John Lewis Way S., 615/577-7711, https://hatchshowprint.com). Hatch Show Print is known for its concert posters, which it's been printing since 1879. During a behind-the-scenes experience at the shop ($20 adults, $15 kids), you can learn about letterpress printing and even bring home your own creation. Hatch's iconic letterpress style is hailed as one of the most iconic looks in modern design. They continue to design and print handouts, posters, and T-shirts for local and national customers.

Part of Hatch Show Print is the small **Haley Gallery,** which offers historical restrikes of original posters from the Hatch Show Print collection, as well as contemporary interpretations

Local Lore

The shape of the rotunda that houses the Hall of Fame is intended to evoke a silo, recalling those that dot rural landscapes. The design is a nod to the rural roots of country music. The four discs on the rotunda's roof show the evolution of recordings from the 78 to the LP, to the 45, and finally to the CD. (I suppose it was hard to visually demonstrate a digital download....)

of the shop's classic wood blocks, created by local and national artists. (A restrike involves using the original blocks and plates to reproduce an image.) The contemporary works here are interpretations of the Hatch style of classic prints; usually works on paper, but sometimes jewelry and decorative objects, too. If you're looking for a fine art piece, rather than the knockoffs that line Broadway, this is a must-stop.

Connect with...

7 Kick up your heels at a honky-tonk

12 Go backstage at the Ryman Auditorium

26 Rhapsodize about your favorites at music museums

31 Make your eyes water sampling hot chicken

Why Go: No food has become as synonymous with Nashville as hot chicken. Plus, it'll clear your sinuses.

Where: There's hardly a Nashville neighborhood without hot chicken these days.

Timing: There's no bad time to eat hot chicken. In winter the spices warm you up; in summer they make you forget about the sweltering heat because your internal thermostat goes through the roof. The **Music City Hot Chicken Festival** each year on July 4 is the best place to compare and contrast lots of different recipes.

The story of hot chicken begins like this: In the 1930s, a Nashville woman was tired of her boyfriend stepping out on her. One night she'd had enough and decided to make his favorite fried chicken extra spicy as punishment. But it turned out that he *liked* it extra hot. Her name, in one of the great travesties of culinary history, has been lost to time. But the man with the roving eye, Thornton Prince, took the idea and ran with it, eventually opening **Prince's Hot Chicken Shack** (5814 Nolensville Pike, 615/810-9388, www.princeshotchicken.com) in the 1940s. As the originator, Prince's is still considered the gold standard for hot chicken today. And it doesn't hurt that its secret recipe is spicy beyond compare. Prince's great niece, André Prince Jeffries, runs the restaurant now, which includes multiple locations.

A former cook at Prince's, Bolton Polk had a disagreement with his bosses and opened his own joint in the 1980s. Polk passed along his recipe, which is heavy on pepper, to his nephew, Bolton Matthews. The small shack closed when Polk died, but Matthews and partner Dollye Ingram reopened in East Nashville in 1997 and expanded **Bolton's Spicy Chicken & Fish** (624 Main St., 615/254-8015, www.boltonsspicy.com) into a restaurant with a lovely patio, along with other locations. Sadly, Bolton passed away in 2021. Dollye still owns the business.

Former Nashville mayor Bill Purcell was a fan of hot chicken, and once referred to Prince's as his "second office." He's partly responsible for introducing the world to Nashville's specialty. As Purcell's second term was ending in 2007, he started the **Music City Hot Chicken Festi-**

▲ Hattie B's Hot Chicken

▲ Prince's Hot Chicken Shack

▲ Hattie B's Hot Chicken

▲ Bolton's Spicy Chicken & Fish

val (www.hot-chicken.com) in East Nashville. The idea was for the city's hot chicken purveyors to show off their chops, allowing people to sample the various spicy secret recipes—and it worked. Hot chicken became a national obsession.

Traditionally, hot chicken is pan-fried and served bone-in on a plate with a slice of Wonder bread (to give you a little break from the heat) and a pickle chip on top. Order it as spicy as you can take it, but not so hot that you can't enjoy the flavor. Some places offer as many as eight different levels of spice; if you're a first timer, try somewhere in the middle. If you're at a spot that's offering their hot chicken as a dare, rather than a dish, go somewhere else. You want to be able to taste it.

Today, a growing number of spots specialize in this local dish. There are casual joints, like Prince's, that just serve hot chicken. There are high-end restaurants that put their twist on it. Here's a cross-section of choices with different flavor profiles, drink menus, and options for vegetarians:

Hattie B's Hot Chicken (112 19th Ave. S., 615/678-4794, http://hattieb.com) has become one of the city's most popular hot chicken purveyors. Hattie B's offers vegetarian sides and beer in an air-conditioned space. They also accept credit cards, which is not the case at many of the city's mom-and-pop shacks.

Party Fowl (719 8th Ave. S., 615/624-8255, http://partyfowl.com) has quite the claim to fame: Their spice recipe is what Lay's used when they made a hot-chicken potato chip. Party Fowl serves beers and boozy slushies and has lots of TVs playing sports, so it's a good choice for a group that wants to hang out, rather than just eat and go.

Aqui Hines, owner of **400 Degrees** (3704 Clarksville Pk., 615/244-4467, http://400degreeshotchicken.com), is a Nashville native who was an almost daily customer at Prince's until she developed her own recipe. Her hot chicken has a crispy crust because she uses a deep fryer, rather than pan-frying.

Locals in the know swear by the hot chicken served at **Scoreboard Bar & Grill** (2408 Music Valley Dr., 615/883-3866, www.scoreboardbar.net), an otherwise nondescript sports bar in Music Valley. The menu includes hot chicken served on waffles as well as classic white bread.

If you're looking for a unique take on hot chicken, local chefs deliver. Hot chicken *pakora* are on the menu at **Chauhan Ale & Masala House** (123 12th Ave. N., 615/242-8426, http://chauhannashville.com), while **Pelican & Pig** (1010 Gallatin Pike, 615/730-6887, www.pelicanandpig.com) created hot chicken cheese (it's made with duck fat, so it's not vegetarian). **The Southern V** (1200 Buchanan St., 615/802-8136, http://eatatthesouthernv.square.site) serves a vegan take on hot chicken that's made with seitan.

Nashvillians know two truths about their city's specialty: The way to quench the heat of too-spicy chicken is to chase it with milk (it's on the menu at most hot chicken joints for that very reason). And, whatever you do, don't wear mascara when you go eat this eye-watering dish.

Connect with...

6 Celebrate Black culture and history on Jefferson Street

33 Lunch at an old-timer restaurant

32 Get hands-on at kid-friendly museums

Families and Kids • Art and Culture • Be a Tourist in Your City

Why Go: At these kid-friendly museums, the whole family can experience Nashville's creative side.

Where: Downtown and South Nashville are the two parts of the city with the best concentration of family-friendly museums.

Timing: Pick a weekday to have room to run, play, and get one-on-one time with the equipment and exhibits. Several of the museums listed here have special classes and workshops; advance reservations may be required.

People come to Nashville to play music, make art, and express themselves in many other creative ways. Kids, too, can get in on that soul-affirming action at a handful of museums that encourage creativity and exploration.

At the **Tennessee State Museum** (1000 Rosa L. Parks Blvd., 615/741-2692, www.tn.gov/museum) there is a vibrant children's gallery geared toward kids ages 3-8. Designed by artist Lucie Rice, the gallery is a mammoth bright and colorful space where interactive exhibits allow kids to learn about quilt-making in the tradition of Tennessee's artisans, and listen to music from Elvis Presley and Dolly Parton as they explore different parts of the state. A museum staffer will help your kids engage with the space, providing coloring pages and leading them through other activities. The museum occasionally has special events for people with sensory sensitivities; check the website for details. The building affords great views of the adjacent Bicentennial Mall and easy access to the Nashville Farmers Market, a good place for a post-museum lunch.

Railroad enthusiasts should make a trip to the **Tennessee Central Railway Museum** (220 Willow St., 615/244-9001, www.tcry.org), which houses an extensive collection of railroad equipment, paraphernalia, and a jaw-dropping model railroad. Dedicated volunteers restore and care for the collection and are more than willing to chat with kids about railways as they run the miniature trains on their elaborate indoor loops, complete with sound effects and mov-

▲ Tennessee Central Railway Museum

▲ Lane Motor Museum

TENNESSEE-MADE MUSIC TO THE WORLD

Generations built Tennessee's rich musical heritage. Radio station broadcasts and variety shows like the Grand Ole Opry drew gifted performers—and eventually recording studios—to Tennessee.

Over time, Tennessee's music industry grew more diverse. Already home to the blues, Memphis attracted fans worldwide with rock and roll and soul. Rhythm and blues clattered in Nashville before the city was known for country music. Musicians have continued to cast the sounds of Tennessee around the world.

▲ Tennessee State Museum

ing lift bridges. The museum may be best known for the special rail excursions that it runs on the Nashville and Eastern Railroad. Part tour and part performance, the trips feature themes like Old West-style shootouts or the Polar Express and invite passengers to interact with costumed characters on board. The types of train cars vary depending on the trip, but one usually doubles as a gift shop and another as a concession stand (though you're welcome to bring your own food on the train), all pulled by a diesel engine. Kids (and parents) can check out all the different parts of the train, including the caboose. Trips sell out early, particularly for the Polar Express, so book your tickets well in advance.

Car buffs and curious kids alike relish coming to the **Lane Motor Museum** (702 Murfreesboro Pike, 615/742-7445, www.lanemotormuseum.org). Here, you'll find all manner of automobiles, from early hybrids and steam engines, to a car that's so small it can be reversed merely by picking it up with a lever and putting it down facing the other direction. The amphibious cars are always a delight, too. (They don't go underwater inside the museum, but there are small screens that show how they work.) The museum has the largest collection of European cars and motorcycles in the country; it's so big that not everything is on display at all times. These cars are no-touch, so little fingers need to stay behind the ropes, but kids will enjoy the museum-led demos, display videos, and the fantastical nature of the place. There's a play area for smaller kids who want to let off some steam, with auto-themed climbing equipment and plastic toys. Glass dividers allow you to watch the restoration of antique automobiles in progress, which is a particular draw for kids who like to see how things work.

No place in Music City is about hands-on science education as much as the **Adventure Science Center** (800 Fort Negley Blvd., 615/862-5160, www.adventuresci.org). Interactive exhibits explore how the body works, the complexities of the solar system, and other scientific topics. Perhaps the most popular attraction is the multistory climbing tower in the building's center, adorned with a giant guitar and other instruments. The center's **Sudekum Planetarium** is the largest planetarium in Tennessee. It has 164 seats and offers a variety of space-themed shows. It also includes gravity-suspending rides and exhibits about spaceflight, the moon, and the solar system.

The upstairs of the **Frist Art Museum** (919 Broadway, 615/244-3340, http://fristartmuseum.org) is the **Martin ArtQuest Gallery,** a hands-on art space for kids—from toddlers to preteens—and their parents. Activities in the Martin ArtQuest Gallery are often tied to the Frist's current special exhibits and use mediums like paint, pencil, digital animation, and sculpture to engage kids with the topic at hand. The Frist is housed in an old Art Deco post office (you can still mail letters in the basement), and its building and grounds are great for family-friendly exploration. The Frist also offers trilingual (English, Spanish, and ASL) story time once a month. Multisensory tours of the museum, which include verbal descriptions as well as scent and tactile experiences, are available with an advance appointment.

Taylor Swift signed her first record contract at the **Country Music Hall of Fame and Museum** (222 Rep. John Lewis Way/5th Ave. S., 615/416-2001, http://countrymusichalloffame. org). Maybe that's why she donated $4 million to start the **Taylor Swift Education Center,** an interactive space upstairs at the hall of fame where kids and parents can think creatively about songwriting and music-making. The center hosts scheduled programming where you might learn to play an instrument or build your own out of non-traditional materials. Classes are geared toward everyone from toddlers to teens, plus some adult-only options, so you're likely to find something that works for your family.

Connect with...

18 Celebrate Latin America at Plaza Mariachi

21 Play with your food at family-friendly restaurants

33 Lunch at an old-timer restaurant

Food

Why Go: Sometimes, with the excitement of a celebrity chef, Nashville's stalwarts get overlooked. These restaurants have been open 60 years or more, which is no small feat.

Where: You'll find an old-timer in almost every city neighborhood, with a concentration downtown and near Vanderbilt University.

Timing: There's a lot of lunch-time strength on this list, so set aside a couple of hours midday for a feast (and then a nap).

The oldest restaurant in Tennessee, **Varallo's Chili Parlor & Restaurant** (239 4th Ave. N., 615/256-1907, www.varallosrestaurants.com) is a throwback to another era, when chili parlors dotted the city streets the way burger joints do today. The restaurant was owned and run by members of the Varallo family from 1907 to 2019, when it was sold to a longtime employee. They still adhere to the original 1907 recipes, resulting in a three-way chili that is similar in style to Cincinnati chili, but with chunks of Mississippi Delta tamales. Varallo's features a cafeteria line, similar to a meat-and-three. You pick your dishes (with or without chili) and carry your tray to a table. Varallo's is open for breakfast and lunch on weekdays only and attracts the downtown worker crowd.

Since 1910, **Capitol Grille** (231 6th Ave. N., 615/244-3121, www.thehermitagehotel.com), tucked inside the historic Hermitage Hotel, has been one of the preferred places for the city's elite movers-and-shakers. Many of the city's best-known chefs got their start here. The restaurant manages its own farm, Glen Leven, about 10 minutes away, meaning the heirloom produce couldn't be fresher. They also maintain their own herd of cattle; the meat is humanely processed and high quality. It's rumored that the restaurant will be renovated and renamed soon. But no matter who the chef is, what's on the menu, or how the decor has been updated, one thing is for sure: It's a swanky spot to rub elbows with politicians, theatergoers, and others looking for a good cocktail and a satisfying meal.

The Loveless Cafe

Wendell Smith's

Elliston Place Soda Shop

A dive bar with tasty cheeseburgers and the oldest beer license in Nashville, **Brown's Diner** (2102 Blair Blvd., 615/269-5509), first opened in 1927, is the very definition of unassuming. These modest paneled walls and low ceilings have long welcomed guests to dine without pretension; being here is like hanging out in your parents' basement with your best friends. In late 2020, Brown's longtime owner sold the iconic burger stop to Bret Tuck, who had been a chef at Edley's BBQ. Tuck is committed to keeping things just as good as ever.

Elliston Place Soda Shop (2015 Elliston Pl., 615/327-1090, www.ellistonplacesodashop.com) is an old-fashioned soda foundation, straight out of the movies. It opened in 1939, closed in 2020, then re-opened next door in 2021. While the decor is new, it has the original aesthetic and menu, with better quality ingredients, more space, and a walk-up window for grabbing a milkshake to go. The menu includes meat-and-three-style dishes (delivered to your retro booth), pimento cheese, fried pickles, and burgers. There are also homemade pies by the slice—and whole to take home. The delicious milkshakes come in flavors like Butterfinger,

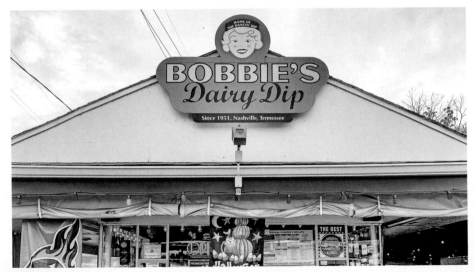
▲ Bobbie's Dairy Dip

pineapple, and classic chocolate malts. The shop sometimes hosts live music performances from a small stage.

Wendell Smith's (5300 Charlotte Ave., 615/383-7114, www.wendellsmithsrestaurant. net) has one of the most iconic neon signs in town, promising "fine food" and imploring you to "eat" in oversized green font. Since 1952 this West Nashville meat-and-three has served old-fashioned home-style cooking in a diner environment. Dishes include tomatoes stuffed with tuna salad, burgers, and full breakfasts. Right across the street is **Bobbie's Dairy Dip** (5301 Charlotte Ave.), which, since 1951, has been the city's favorite place for milkshakes, ice cream, and other summertime dessert favorites. Bobbie's has limited winter hours, opening when the weather warrants.

The Loveless Cafe (8400 Hwy. 100, 615/646-9700, www.lovelesscafe.com) got its start in 1951 when Lon and Annie Loveless began serving country cooking to travelers on Highway 100. Over the years the restaurant changed hands, but Annie's biscuit recipe has remained the same—and it's those biscuits that keep Nashvillians coming back for more. Some locals grumble that tourists and time have made Loveless different from what it once was. But the biscuits are fluffy and buttery, the ham salty, and the eggs, bacon, and sausage will hit the spot. You'll know you're close when you see the large blue neon sign. The Loveless is 150 yards from the northern terminus of the Natchez Trace Parkway.

While no one knows the exact date it opened, it's impossible to talk about Nashville's storied, long-time restaurants without mentioning **Prince's Hot Chicken Shack** (5814 Nolensville Pike, 615/810-9388, www.princeshotchicken.com). Open since the 1940s, it paved the way for hundreds of interpretations (and imitations) of its legendary hot chicken. André Prince Jeffries, the great-niece of the man who first took the idea and ran with it, now runs the restaurant's chicken empire, which also includes multiple outposts. The casual spot on Nolensville Pike has a small patio and TVs inside where you can watch whatever game is on while you wait for your pan-fried hot chicken.

Connect with...

🟤 Make your eyes water sampling hot chicken
🟤 Drive the Natchez Trace Parkway

34 Go to Nashville Fashion Week in style

Shopping

Why Go: Music City is all about creativity and looking good, so a whole week focused on fashion is great fun—and great eye candy. If you think Nashville Fashion Week is all rhinestones and blue jeans, you'll be pleasantly surprised.

Where: Events all around town • www.nashvillefashionweek.com

Timing: Fashion Week typically takes place in March; many events, such as the runway shows and gala, are at night.

Nashville Fashion Week was started in 2010 and modeled after New York Fashion Week. Since then, NFW has been presenting runway shows by local designers and drawing the who's who of the fashion industry to town. The highest profile events of the week are the four nights of runway shows, featuring collections that run the gamut from high fashion to high fun, embracing the city's entrepreneurial, creative spirit. Because this is Nashville, many of the shows have high production values and feature live music from well-known artists. Many of the runway shows take place at **OZ Arts** (6172 Cockrill Bend Cir., 615/350-7200, www.ozartsnashville. org), a performance space on the west side. Tickets tend to cost $50-75 (some are standing room only). Some events sell out, but you should be able to snag a ticket to what you want to see.

In addition to seeing pretty creations on the catwalk, you can also attend educational sessions, from panel discussions about getting into the industry to photography classes and jewelry-making workshops. And it wouldn't be Fashion Week without a gala. This ticketed event features a seated dinner, more fashion on display, and opportunities to meet participating designers. The gala raises funds for grants for up-and-coming Middle Tennessee designers and others in the industry. It's a fun event to dress up for—creative looks are appreciated in this crowd.

Even though NFW is just a week long, you can celebrate year-round. Some of the designers and brands whose looks have been integral to Fashion Week have boutiques you can visit:

Nashville Fashion Week

Nashville Fashion Week runway model

runway show finale at Nashville Fashion Week

Known for using sequins in nearly all his creations, Andrew Clancey moved his store **Any Old Iron** (8 Music Sq., 917/912-0470, www.anyoldiron.us) from New York to Nashville's Music Row in 2014. He's dressed Taylor Swift, Lady Gaga, Beyoncé, Cardi B, Miranda Lambert, and many prominent Nashvillians who enjoy the sparkly stuff.

Look for jewelry, clothing, and leather goods like purses and shoes at **ABLE** (5022 Centennial Blvd., 615/723-4836, www.livefashionable.com) in The Nations. The fashion brand is focused on ethical production processes and paying a living wage to its workers. ABLE's simple, streamlined handbags are seen all around town.

Judith Bright (2307 12th Ave. S., 615/269-5600, http://judithbright.com) sells semi-custom wire-wrapped jewelry often worn by big-screen actresses. The necklaces, rings, bracelets, and earrings can be made with different gemstones and finishes and are popular among bridesmaids who want coordinating pieces. Bright and her staff make and customize the pieces onsite. In addition to the shop in 12South, the brand has a second location in Franklin.

Ethan Summers is the founder, lead designer, and owner of **Oil/Lumber** (2100 Dunn Ave., 801/814-8375, www.oilandlumber.com), a brand that sells both furniture and men's and women's clothing with an eye toward sustainability. Summers originally came to Nashville to play college soccer, but he stuck around after forging connections with the local creative community. It's worth checking out the minimalist workshop in Wedgewood-Houston, a unique spot that makes handcrafted unisex jackets as well as wood coffee tables and chairs. It's open to the public, but appointments are required.

Some of Music City's designers don't have physical shops, but they do have websites where you can buy their creations.

Amanda Valentine (www.amandavalentine.com) has appeared on several seasons of *Project Runway* and is known for dressing rock stars. Her designs are known for their bright patterns and bold color blocking.

Black by Maria Silver (https://blackbymariasilver.com) is clothing that's designed by and for musicians. Silver works with a diverse group of models to show her ethical, size-inclusive designs.

Hailey Lane incorporates vintage Parisian elements into her pieces for **H. Lane Design**

some of the designs during Nashville Fashion Week

(https://hlanedesign.com). Look for vintage lace and other accents in her clutches, scarves, and clothing.

Jamie + the Jones (https://jamieandthejones.com) is owned by childhood friends Jamie Frazier and Hannah Jones. The silk and other natural fibers used in the flowing, ephemeral clothing, are made in the United States.

Textile designer Andra Eggleston, who runs **Electra Eggleston** (www.electraeggleston.com), is the daughter of famous artist William Eggleston. Some of her collections build off of his paintings.

Connect with...

⓯ Create a masterpiece at a makerspace
㉘ Treat yourself to custom-made boots

35 Wander the Buchanan Arts District

Neighborhoods and City Streets • Art and Culture • Shopping

Why Go: The energy of this North Nashville neighborhood is palpable, making it a fun place to shop, see art, and listen to jazz.

Where: The Buchanan Arts District is bounded by I-65 on the east and Dr. DB Todd Jr. Boulevard on the west.

Timing: Stroll around in the afternoon, stopping into shops and galleries, then admire the neighborhood's murals during golden hour, just before sunset.

The Buchanan Arts District, which comprises Buchanan Street and a few blocks surrounding it, is a mural-filled neighborhood in North Nashville that's known as being a hub of creativity and independence. Businesses like **Bud's Hardware and Key Shop** (1600 Buchanan St., 615/256-6524) have anchored Buchanan Street since the 1960s, encouraging a community of makers and DIYers. So, it's no surprise that innovative businesses and arts venues have been drawn here over the years.

Three childhood friends opened **Slim & Husky's Pizza Beeria** (911 Buchanan St., 615/561-1787, http://slimandhuskys.com) in 2017. The trio transformed the concept of custom artisan pizza into a thriving chain. Now the restaurant has a number of other locations; in 2021, Slim & Husky's became the first Black-owned business on Broadway. The team also owns **The Rollout** (1006 Buchanan St., 615/647-7017), a shop across the street that sells creatively topped cinnamon rolls.

Salemtown Board Co./Maple Built (1003 Buchanan St., www.maplebuilt.com) builds custom skateboards and teaches youth from low-income communities woodworking skills (to use on skateboards or to make other goods). The shop is a funky, bright space that displays its boards like the works of art they are. Even if you're not a skateboarder, it's worth going in and admiring the boards and the handcrafted wood furniture. Outside is a colorfully painted skate ramp to try out your gear.

▲ Slim & Husky's Pizza Beeria

▲ The Rollout

▲ Nashville Jazz Workshop

▴ Elephant Gallery

Since 2000, the **Nashville Jazz Workshop** (1012 Buchanan St., 615/242-5299, http://
nashvillejazz.org) has been proving that Music City isn't only about country music. At its headquarters on Buchanan, the nonprofit hosts acoustic jazz performances, as well as teaching
classes and workshops for all ages. The 72-seat Jazz Cave, where most of the shows take place,
also features local artwork. Tickets are sold online or from the on-site box office.

At **Elephant Gallery** (1411 Buchanan St., www.elephantgallery.com), sculptor Alex
Lockwood exhibits thought-provoking works from local and regional artists, including many
BIPOC artists. The airy front room functions as the main exhibition space. The back rooms
include studios for artists and classrooms for public workshops. You'll know you're in the right
place when you see the whimsical horned creature sculpture, by Brett Douglas Hunter, in front
of the green building.

The murals of **Norf Art Collective** (http://norfstudios.com) can be seen on the sides of
multiple buildings in the area. At 26th Avenue North and Clarksville Pike is *Family Matters,*
which depicts Diane Nash, Z. Alexander Looby, John Lewis, and other prominent Civil Rights

Local Lore

Head less than a mile west to where Buchanan Street meets Ed Temple Boulevard and you'll spot a colorful retro sign for the **Eldorado Motel** (2806 Ed Temple Dr.), marking an otherwise empty lot. From its opening in the 1950s, the motel was listed in the Green Book as a place where Black travelers could safely stay the night. In its day, both Martin Luther King Jr. and Harry Belafonte slept here. The sign stands near Ted Rhodes Golf Course, which was named for the Black professional golfer who lived at the Eldorado late in his life. While the motel was leveled in 2012, local preservation groups have worked to ensure the sign stays where it is.

leaders. On a wall of Slim & Husky's is an ode to Spike Lee's *School Daze*. (Norf also created much of the signage for Slim & Husky's and The Rollout.) At 1114 Buchanan Street is my personal favorite, ***And her hair was an unfolded flower,*** depicting the profile of a Black woman whose hair flows the length of the building.

The neighborhood also features some wearable art. Spacious, airy **Nisolo** (1803 9th Ave. N., 615/953-1087, http://nisolo.com) sells fair trade men's and women's shoes made by Peruvian craftspeople. The options run the gamut from sneakers to Oxfords to sandals. The showroom is crisp and simple, so that the shoes are the focus—and rightfully so.

Connect with...

6 Celebrate Black culture and history on Jefferson Street

25 Feed your mind in North Nashville

36 Taste the international flavors of Nolensville Pike

Food • Neighborhoods and City Streets

Why Go: Many immigrant communities have made Nashville their home. Sample from the countless cuisines on Nolensville Pike, the city's most international street.

Where: Nolensville Pike runs diagonally from downtown. The places covered here start about 3 miles southeast of downtown and span 8 more miles south. It's easiest to drive (free parking is plentiful), but you could also use Lyft or take the number 52 bus.

Timing: Several of these restaurants are essentially delis inside markets and are open for breakfast, lunch, and dinner. I like weekday lunches here best, because I can browse the shops and markets before or after I eat.

Much of Nashville's foreign-born population has settled along Nolensville Pike, the busy street that leads from downtown through the southeast side of the city. It's home to significant Kurdish, Latinx, Somalian, Djiboutian, and Ethiopian communities, as well as people hailing from several nations in West Africa and Asia.

The street is a strip of businesses, from vintage stores to flag shops, where inflatable animals perch on rooftops and street art pops up seemingly overnight. The smell of cooking food wafts down the sidewalk, beckoning you to dine from an incredible array of cuisines. No matter what you're hungry for, you can probably find it here. The spots covered here are organized from north to south, starting with the ones closest to downtown.

InterAsian Market and Deli (2160 Nolensville Pike, 615/742-3268, http://interasian-market.com) is a wonderland of Vietnamese and Laotian foods, including banh mi sandwiches and steamed buns. Local chefs swear by the pork belly. Occasionally they offer pop-up specials of *banh knot* (a sweet and savory rice cake) and egg rolls. InterAsian has been a fixture of Nashville since 1994. The market also sells groceries and fresh-made meals to go.

Just off of Nolensville Pike, **Gojo Ethiopian Café and Restaurant** (415 W. Thompson Ln., 615/332-0710, http://gojoethiopiancafe.com) serves lamb and beef dishes as well as vege-

▲ Casa Azafrán

▲ Azafrán Park

163

tarian offerings. Highlights include the chicken curry and peas and the *kik aletcha* (yellow split peas with fresh ginger).

You'll know **Carniceria y Taqueria Don Juan** (2910 Nolensville Pike, 615/833-1690) when you walk by its colorful mural depicting a Mexican street scene (its menu is also painted on the same wall). The small restaurant serves chicken and pork tamales and ribs, but it's their tacos that draw crowds. If you really fall in love with the barbecue meats, you can buy some by the pound.

Salvadoran restaurant **Pupuseria Reina La Bendicion** (3003 Nolensville Pike, 615/243-8425) is tucked away in the back half of the building it's in. (Look for the bright blue wall, which you can see from Timmons Street.) Pupusas, which are thick cornmeal cakes filled with pork, cheese, or eggs, are the signature dish.

A *michoacana* is a traditional Mexican *paleta* shop, and yes, you can find refreshing fruit popsicles at **La Michoacana Premium** (3763 Nolensville Pike, 615/457-1385). But what people come here for are the Dorilocos, a playful and spicy snack with ice cream, Japanese peanuts, and hot sauce piled in a single-serve Doritos bag, chips and all.

Farther south, approaching Harding Place, you'll pass **Little Kurdistan** and its collection of restaurants. Kurdish cuisine isn't the only Middle Eastern culinary tradition on the street, though. **King Tut's** (3716 Nolensville Pike, 615/944-3735, http://kingtutsnashville. com) is a popular food truck serving what's arguably Nashville's best falafel, as well as chicken shawarma and gyros. Permanently parked on Nolensville, the truck is adjacent to a relaxing, plant-bedecked patio.

Nestled in an unassuming strip mall, **Taj Indian Restaurant** (3943 Nolensville Pike, 615/750-3490, www.tajnashville.com) offers Indian and Indo-Chinese food, including tandoori, and both vegetarian and vegan dishes. The lunch buffet is a favorite of people who work in the neighborhood.

Subculture Urban Cuisine and Café (5737 Nolensville Pike, 615/955-1223, http://subculturecafe.com) is a tiny space with just a few tables both indoors and out. What's not small is its menu of street foods—think tacos, empanadas, and other easy-to-carry bites—from a variety of Latin American cuisines. Favorite sandwiches include the Cubano with pulled pork and the vegetarian *churrasco* (made with a fried egg, avocado, and chimichurri sauce).

Community Focus

In 2014, former President Barack Obama spoke about immigration reform at the community center **Casa Azafrán** (2105 Nolensville Pike, 615/320-5152, www.casaazafran. org). More than 10 different organizations that support immigrants operate out of the center. Marked by a vibrant mosaic entrance, it's also home to **Azafrán Park,** an outdoor area with a splash park and play equipment, and **Mesa Komal,** a community kitchen used by locals to run their food businesses.

If you like to cook at your table, settle in at **Sichuan Hot Pot & Asian Cuisine** (5680 Nolensville Pike, 615/750-2582, www.hotpotnashville.com). You'll be served a boiling pot of broth and in it you'll cook your choice of shrimp, meat, and vegetables, while dining in a room decorated with a giant horse sculpture and a babbling fountain. Some of the tables are even covered by pagodas.

Of course, Nolensville Pike has attractions other than food. Whenever I'm in the area, I like to poke around at antiques shop **Decent Folk Vintage** (2523B Nolensville Pike, 615/942-8490, www.decentfolkvintage.com) and **Totally Rad Toyhouse** (2519 Nolensville Pike, 615/602-3153, www.totallyradtoyhouse.com), which sells retro toys. Just around the corner, **Craft South** (410 Woodbine St., 615/928-8766, www.craft-south.com) is stocked with everything a fiber artist could wish for, including fabric, yarn, and thread.

Connect with...

18 Celebrate Latin America at Plaza Mariachi

27 Feast on Kurdish food

37 Lace up your boots for an urban hike

Outdoor Adventures • Families and Kids

Why Go: Nashville's greenways offer easy access to solitude and scenic views by way of a variety of hiking trails—and you don't have to venture far to enjoy them.

Where: Locations include Beaman Park, 11 miles northwest of downtown; Whites Creek, 11 miles north of downtown; and Bells Bend; 15 miles west of downtown • 615/862-8400, https://greenwaysfornashville.org

Timing: Go on a weekday in spring, when the wildflowers are blooming, the creeks are burbling, and you have the trails to yourself.

Nashville and Middle Tennessee tend to be overlooked when it comes to the outdoors. It's the state's other regions that are so well known for recreation: Memphis has the Mississippi River. East Tennessee has the Smokies. Chattanooga has the Ocoee River and a pair of mountains. But Middle Tennessee deserves your attention, too, with miles of lush parks, curving rivers and creeks, and placid lakes. Thanks to the city's impressive system of greenways, it couldn't be easier to experience the great outdoors here.

Organized around the area's eight major water corridors, the greenways cover about 100 miles in total and are largely paved. But there are also "primitive trails"—dirt paths that make you feel like you're deep in the wilderness even if you're steps from a major commercial center or street.

Beaman Park (4255 Little Marrowbone Rd., 615/862-8580) is the jewel of the system for its varied ecosystems of wetlands, meadows, and forest. Once called Paradise Ridge, this park occupies 2,371 acres, with unpaved greenway trails that include some significant elevation changes. One of those is the rolling 2.2-mile **Henry Hollow Loop,** which boasts several pretty overlooks, meandering creeks, and lots of shade. To spend more time immersed in the forest and admiring wildflowers, take Henry Hollow to the **Ridgetop Trail** for a five-mile jaunt. For a flatter stroll, just wander alongside Henry Creek, turning around when you're ready. The park is half an hour north of downtown.

▲ Beaman Park

▲ Shelby Bottoms Greenway

At the lesser-known **Whites Creek Greenway Trails at Fontanel** (4225 Whites Creek Pike) are two connected loops that give a glimpse of some Music City history on a lovely property. The relatively flat, 1.5-mile paved loop is wheelchair- and stroller-friendly, offering views of the hillside, meadows, and Fontanel, once the estate of country music star Barbara Mandrell (now a multiuse development). The paved trails connect to a steeper 1.8-mile dirt loop that winds its way on narrow trails behind Mandrell's old mansion, once the largest log cabin in the world. Despite the development nearby, this is a remote hike that grants access to pristine wilderness. Whites Creek is just east of US 431, about 20 minutes north from downtown.

Old farm roads have been turned into wide, flat trails at **Bells Bend Park** (4107 Old Hickory Blvd.). The 808 acres here, set on a bend in the Cumberland River, are home to migratory birds and blooming meadows. Park at the **Poplar Hollow Trailhead** and take one of several overlapping loops; there are 7.4 miles of unpaved trails. Bells Bend is also popular with mountain bikers and has 5.5 miles of bike trails. The **Bells Bend Nature Center** (4187 Old

▲ Whites Creek Greenway Trails at Fontanel

Hickory Blvd., 615/862-4187) runs family-friendly programming to encourage kids to get out on the trails. The park is about half an hour west of downtown.

On the east side of town is **Shelby Bottoms Greenway** (1900 Shelby Bottoms Greenway, 615/862-8539). Its proximity to downtown and the Opryland complex means you won't find complete solitude here, but with 6.6 miles of unpaved trails, it is possible to go on a secluded hike in the middle of the city. From the Forrest Green entrance, follow the **Cornelia Fort Trail** to **Fox Trail** or the **Native Grounds Trail** for a loop that includes meadows, blackberry bushes, and lots of deer, owls, and birds. This route connects to a major paved greenway (part of the **Music City Bikeway**), which you can follow to the Shorebird and Wildlife Habitat Pond at the base of the Cumberland Pedestrian Bridge. The paved sections are wheelchair- and stroller-accessible and tend to be more crowded than the dirt trails.

Note that while the city's greenways are largely barrier-free, restrooms and port-a-johns may not be accessible.

When you're ready for more, just open the map and point. Chances are you won't be too far from a greenway.

Connect with...

5 Pedal the Music City Bikeway

22 Get the best views of the city

38 Taste Tennessee's bounty at U-Pick-Em farms

Outdoor Adventures • Families and Kids • Food • Day Trips

Why Go: Nothing tastes better than a peach, apple, or handful of berries that you picked yourself. Head to one of Middle Tennessee's U-Pick-Em farms to get your produce straight from the source.

Where: You don't have to go far beyond the city—less than an hour—to find agricultural abundance. The farms listed here are to the east, west, and south of Nashville.

Timing: Growing season runs from April to October, with strawberries from April to June, blueberries, blackberries, and peaches in June and July, and raspberries in August. Apple season starts in late August and may be wrapped up by Halloween.

Call or check social media for up-to-date info before you head out, as crops vary based on weather. In peak season many farms are open daily, but they scale back their hours as the crops dwindle.

When I host people from out of the country, they always remark on how green Middle Tennessee is. Indeed, Nashville is a lush place—with a major river, state parks, lakes, greenways, and arboretums. But my visitors are also referring to the verdant landscape of Middle Tennessee that surrounds the city, spanning hundreds of miles.

That lush landscape isn't just for admiring. It's also fertile ground for growing fruits, vegetables, and flowers. Take advantage of this bounty by getting in the car (empty the trunk first; a bushel of fruit is bigger than you'd expect) and heading to one of the area farms that welcome you to pick-your-own produce. Many places will let you bring your own baskets, boxes, or bags, but also have containers for sale.

Bring shoes that can get muddy, sunscreen, a hat, and whatever else you need for a good time outdoors. Oh, and bring an empty stomach, because you'll do some sampling on the car ride home. Plus, many farms sell baked goods, jam, honey, and other treats.

The two-generation family-owned **Kelley's Berry Farm** (50 Riverview Estates Ln., Castalian Springs, 615/633-1426, www.kelleysberries.com) is lush with berries to pick from May through September. Head 45 minutes east of Nashville for strawberries, raspberries,

The Peach Truck

blackberries, blueberries, and peaches. The Kelleys sell at several of Nashville's farmers markets. While you're in the area, you can take a tour of the Castalian Springs Mound Site, where a Native American community lived during the Mississippian Period (1000-1450 CE).

In Spring Hill, John and Martha Wagner open their **Wagner Berry Farm** (4923 Ollie Chunn Rd., Spring Hill, 931/486-0036, http://wagnerberry.com) to families and school groups wanting to partake of its cornucopia of color. The couple plants strawberries, raspberries, blackberries, and blueberries to fruit during the summer. In autumn, kids particularly enjoy the pumpkin patch and choosing their own future jack-o'-lanterns. Spring Hill is an easy stop on the way back to Nashville after visiting Columbia.

Not only can you pick strawberries, blackberries, and blueberries at **Circle S Farms** (1627 Old Laguardo Rd. E., Lebanon, 615/405-6860, www.tncirclesfarms.com), you can return in winter and cut your own Christmas tree. Circle S has been in the same family for eight generations, since 1837. Kids like to ride on the tractor-pulled wagon and toy tractors through sand pits. Circle S is an easy drive east on I-40 from Nashville.

▲ Tennessee's rich farmland

Free Fruit

East Nashville's **Shelby Bottoms Greenway** is covered in wild blackberry plants. In early July, those bushes are teeming with fruit and the public is welcome to help themselves. Some years there is even a Metro Parks-sponsored recipe contest to show off what you made. Just limit yourself to one pint per visit and stay on the paths so you don't trample any other plants. Gloves and long sleeves aren't a bad idea, as blackberry plants have thorns.

From June through late autumn, the trees at **Breeden's Orchard** (631 Beckwith Rd., Mt. Juliet, 615/449-2880, http://breedensorchard.com) are full of peaches and then apples. Garlic and berries are sometimes available, too. You can bring Fido with you for the day at the farm as long as he is on a leash.

Thanks to a location close to I-24, **Batey Farm** (5331 Baker Rd., Murfreesboro, 615/848-4116, http://bateyfarms.com) is a popular destination for strawberries and sunflowers. The farm also raises pigs, so bacon is available for your at-home breakfasts.

Fruits are sweet, but if you crave something else, fill your bags with kale, beans, broccoli, lettuce, and other greens, and flowers at **Edens' Garden Farm** (513 Elkmont Pl., Pegram, 615/662-8390). Root crops round out the autumn season. The farm is close to Narrows of the Harpeth, a popular summer canoeing destination that's part of Harpeth River State Park.

If you can't get to a U-Pick-Em farm, but you still want farm-fresh fruit, check out **The Peach Truck** (900 E. Trinity Ln., 615/913-4225, https://thepeachtruck.com) in the city's Inglewood neighborhood. The Nashville-owned company has their orchards in Georgia, so you won't actually be picking these peaches yourself. In the early days, they brought their peaches to farmers markets in a vintage truck. You might not always luck out and see this piece of automotive eye candy, but you will get close-to-fresh-picked peaches, with varieties that vary weekly, and good information about how to ripen your off-the-tree gems.

39 Kayak and paddleboard on Percy Priest Lake

Outdoor Adventures • Day Trips

Why Go: The largest and closest body of water to downtown Nashville, Percy Priest is the place to live the lake life: canoeing, kayaking, paddleboarding, boating, fishing, and swimming.

Where: There are lots of entry points to this 42-mile-long lake. Great options for paddling include Hamilton Creek Recreation Area (13 miles west of downtown); Vivrette Creek (17 miles east of downtown); Long Hunter State Park (25 miles west of downtown)

Timing: The lake's core recreation season is April through October, but it's often temperate enough to paddle on Thanksgiving and Christmas. If you're not a football fan, you'll have fall weekends on the lake to yourself, when everyone else is watching the game.

One of my favorite things about hitting the water on Percy Priest is how easy it is. Even on a busy day with lots of Jet Skis and sailboats on the water, it's not hard to find a launching spot near a cove that's a quick drive from the city and with easy parking. On the water, you can hug the craggy, rocky shoreline, away from the water skiers and motorboats. Grey heron squawk if you get too close and fly overhead, tucking in their long legs. The longer you look, the more fish you'll see jumping out of the water, including bass and crappie. Catfish stay close to the bottom, but you can see them when the water is clear.

It took me a while to discover this natural oasis just 10 miles from downtown, a lake so big and with so many different entry points, it would take years to try them all, each one a different experience. The banks are lined with greenery, including cypress trees, with their knees reaching into the water. The trees growing along the rocky shores make you feel like you are deep in the wilderness, not just a handful of miles from the Nashville International Airport. (On your next flight into or out of Music City, look out the window for an aerial view of Percy Priest's craggy boundaries.) If you launch at **Vivrette Creek** (5598 Alvinn Sperry Rd.), you can cross

▲ padddleboarding on Percy Priest Lake

colorful paddlecraft at the lake

paddleboarding on the lake

Local Lore

Percy Priest is not a natural lake. It was made by damming a section of the Cumberland River and its Stones River tributary in 1968. Water levels on the lake vary substantially depending on how much water is let out of the dam. The bottom of the lake is rocky, and local anglers claim that on low water days, if you mapped out all the rocks and coves, you could find a way to walk across it. Personally, I prefer paddling.

the lake to find a small bridge that kayaks and paddleboards can sneak under, too small for motorized boats; the waters on the other side are secluded, with wildlife free for the gazing.

The lake is free of tide and current, but there's enough wind, boat wake, and changing water levels to keep things interesting. Frigid in winter, the water warms up through the summer, until it's bathwater warm by late August. Jumping (or falling) off the paddleboard for a swim is one of the top pleasures of summer.

The majority of Percy Priest paddlers bring their own vessels, but there are a few outfitters who rent gear in the height of summer, including the **Metro Parks Department** (various locations, www.nashville.gov), **Nashville Paddle Co.** (2901 Bell Rd., 615/682-1787, www.nashvillepaddle.com), and at **Long Hunter State Park** (2901 Hobson Pike, Hermitage, 615/885-2422, https://tnstateparks.com). After a long, hot day on the water, stop by one of the waterside restaurants, such as **Shipwreck Cove** (3361 Bell Rd., 615/872-8800, www.shipwreckcovetn.com), for a plate of fried food and an icy drink before heading home.

Connect with...

37 Lace up your boots for an urban hike
38 Taste Tenneesee's bounty at U-Pick-Em farms

40

Sip your way down the Tennessee Whiskey Trail

Day Trips

Why Go: What France is to Champagne and Kentucky is to bourbon, Tennessee is to whiskey. Sample the liquid gold that comes from these hills.

Where: There are distilleries across the state, but the majority are in Middle Tennessee around Nashville.

Timing: Spring and fall are the best bets, as you get pretty landscapes without the extreme summer weather or the crowds.

When in Rome, do as the Romans do. Ergo, when in Tennessee, drink Tennessee whiskey. By definition, this liquor is a bourbon whiskey made in-state. Like bourbon, Tennessee whiskey must be made from at least 51 percent corn and aged in new charred-oak barrels. The difference is that it also needs to be filtered through maple charcoal.

The **Tennessee Whiskey Trail** (www.tnwhiskeytrail.com) spotlights nearly 30 distilleries. Since the stops are spread throughout the state, a good approach is to make a day trip out of it: Pick one distillery and enjoy the surrounding area after your visit. If you want to see a number of distilleries at once, it's best to let someone else do the driving. **Mint Julep Experiences** (mintjuleptours.com) offers tours of area distilleries. You'll be ushered from stop to stop in an air-conditioned bus with snacks and water.

All of these distilleries offer tours, which are generally guided and last 45-90 minutes. Most include the basics about how distilling works, what it takes to turn grain into liquor, and the specifics of the distillery and their whiskey. You're sure to hear some tall tales about bootleggers and moonshine, too. Most offer tastings, but it's possible to enjoy the tours without drinking, thanks to the sheer amount of information and interesting equipment. Many distilleries charge for tours; some recommend buying tickets in advance.

The world-famous **Jack Daniel's Distillery** (133 Lynchburg Hwy., Lynchburg, 931/759-6357, www.jackdaniels.com) is about 90 minutes from the city. Aside from the addition of elec-

Corsair Artisan Distillery

Donut Distillery

Cascade Hollow Distilling Co.

tricity and big crowds, things haven't changed much since 1866, when Jack Daniel registered his whiskey still at a spring near Lynchburg. After your tour, check out the shops of **Lynchburg** and eat lunch at **Miss Mary Bobo's Restaurant** (295 Main St., 931/759-7394), a former boarding house.

The only 90-proof Tennessee whiskey is made by **George Dickel** at **Cascade Hollow Distilling Co.** (1950 Cascade Hollow Rd., Tullahoma, 931/408-2410, www.georgedickel.com). George Dickel distilled his first bottle of whisky (note the Scottish spelling) at Cascade Hollow in 1870. A hollow is a small valley with a creek that's protected from the summer heat. Many distilleries started in such spots because of the source of water. Combine a tour here with a visit to **Old Stone Fort Archeological Park** (732 Stone Fort Dr., Manchester, 931/461-7676, http://tnstateparks.com) for a tranquil day trip to the countryside.

Opened in 2016, **Leiper's Fork Distillery** (3381 Southall Rd., Franklin, 615/465-6456, http://leipersforkdistillery.com) is a newcomer when compared with Daniels and Dickel. This small-batch distillery is Instagram heaven, with its vintage truck in the driveway and rocking chairs on the porch. The whiskey's not bad either. On your tour you'll sit a spell and hear about the process of making their artisan whiskey and bourbon. **Leiper's Fork** is a small town popular with celebrities. Visit the town's antique shops and roadside farm stands after your tour, and keep your eyes peeled for familiar faces.

Old Glory Distilling (451 Alfred Thun Rd., Clarksville, 931/919-2522, http://oldglorydistilling.com) is run by Clarksville locals. Their small-batch whiskeys are aged in half-size barrels, so they take less time to mature. Old Glory also offers a vodka made with the same charcoal-filtering process as their whiskey. This distillery is a good option if you're heading north of Nashville, perhaps en route to Kentucky's Bourbon Trail.

Moonshine is illegally distilled alcohol with mountain roots, known for its gut-punching strength. Folks long made it clandestinely, so they didn't have to pay alcohol taxes. Some distilleries make a legal but still-potent version. It's on the menu along with whiskey at **Short Mountain Distillery** (8289 Short Mountain Rd., Woodbury, 615/563-1243, www.shortmountaindistillery.com). Tours include a walk along Cooper Cave Spring to see the water that makes the magic happen. There's a restaurant on-site, a perfect spot to admire the mountain scenery. Short Mountain is an easy add-on to a trip to **Chattanooga.**

If you're curious about whiskey, but not up for a day trip, there are distilleries in the city, too:

Corsair Artisan Distillery (1200 Clinton St., 615/454-4871, www.corsairdistillery. com) is one of the area's best-known small-batch distilleries. Tours are designed for drinkers and non-drinkers alike and include fresh-baked pizzas. Corsair's headquarters are in Wedgewood-Houston; tours are also available there.

Nelson's Green Brier Distillery (1414 Clinton St., 615/913-8800, http://greenbrierdistillery.com) is close to Corsair. Like Jack Daniel's and George Dickel, this brand was popular in the 1800s. They shut down when Prohibition went into effect, but after 100 years, the founder's descendants reopened the doors and brought back Belle Meade Bourbon in a space with high ceilings and exposed brick walls.

For something completely different, head to East Nashville's **Donut Distillery** (311 Gallatin Ave., 615/678-8685, http://donutdistillery.com) for a signature whiskey-glazed doughnut. The shop has a full bar, so you can also order a whiskey to sip.

Connect with...

㉓ Toast the legacy of Printers Alley

㊹ Climb, bike, and paddle in Chattanooga

41 Go chasing waterfalls

Outdoor Adventures • Day Trips

Why Go: Tennessee has lots of rocky gorges and running rivers, which translates into plenty of waterfalls, including one of the tallest single vertical drops east of the Rocky Mountains.

Where: There are waterfalls across the state, but the best concentration is east and south of Nashville, including on the Cumberland Plateau. The majority are inside state parks, where admission is free.

Timing: Waterfalls are best in spring. As snow melts in the mountains, the water will be at its highest, resulting in roaring falls surrounded by greenery and wildflowers.

Waterfalls are Instagram gold, sure, but they're also good for our brains. The constant movement and sound of the water, like nature's version of white noise, helps us relax. There's even some research that suggests the negative ions released from the falling water encourage the production of serotonin in our brains. So, it's happy news that many Tennessee waterfalls are just a day trip away from the city. Reaching some of these natural wonders requires a strenuous hike and surefootedness; others are more easily accessible from parking lots and flat trails. Here are the top three waterfalls near Nashville:

Cummins Falls (Cummins Falls State Park, 390 Cummins Falls Ln., Cookeville, 931/268-7223, https://tnstateparks.com) is a dramatic tiered cascade of water that plummets down 75 feet into a swimming area. Reach it via a steep, slippery, and challenging hike down into a gorge. Once there, you're surrounded by rock and falling water; it's like stumbling across a utopian grotto. This popular destination is only reachable via permit, which you can obtain online for a small fee. The trails into the gorge are 1-1.5 miles long; due to the difficulty, the hike isn't recommended for kids under 5. Wear a life jacket in the gorge. To take in the beauty of Cummins Falls in a less strenuous way, walk to the overlook that's less than half a mile from the parking area. Look down and see the falls plunging into the pool and hear the rushing water. The path

▲ Burgess Falls State Park

▲ Burgess Falls

Fall Creek Falls State Park

to the overlook is gravel and may not be appropriate for wheelchairs. The park is 80 miles east of downtown Nashville.

You get to hike past four different waterfalls at **Burgess Falls State Park** (8400 Old Cane Creek Rd., Baxter, 931/432-5312, https://tnstateparks.com), including the 136-foot-tall namesake. To see this quartet of natural beauty, you'll embark on a steep 1.5-mile round-trip hike, with lots of creek crossings, rocky outcroppings, and no handrails. The payoff is steep cliffs and plummeting water. Opt for the easier mile-long Ridge Top Trail for a view down into the canyon and waterfall without the elevation changes. The park is 80 miles east of downtown Nashville, about 18 miles south of Cummins Falls.

There are several waterfalls inside **Fall Creek Falls State Park** (2009 Village Camp Rd., Spencer, 423/881-5708, https://tnstateparks.com), including the roaring 256-foot Fall Creek Falls, one of the largest waterfalls in the eastern half of the United States. The water shoots over the rocks, creating a dramatic view from the base of the falls. It's an ambitious hike to reach the bottom of the gorge, on the short but hard Base of the Falls Trail (0.7 mile round-

Local Lore

Several movies have been filmed at Fall Creek Falls State Park, including Disney's live-action adaption of *The Jungle Book, King Kong Lives,* and *Turbo: A Power Rangers Movie.*

trip), which is rocky, but has handrails. Enjoy the grandeur of the falls from above by hiking the Gorge Overlook Trail (2.4 miles round-trip), starting from the Betty Dunn Nature Center. The park is 120 miles southeast of downtown Nashville.

There's no reason to stop looking for waterfalls once you've hit the top three. Tennesseans love the mammoth **South Cumberland State Park** (11745 US 41, Monteagle, 931/924-2989, https://tnstateparks.com) for its challenging hikes, great views, and many waterfalls, including Greeter Falls and Foster Falls, which have deep enough pools for swimming. **Rock Island State Park** (82 Beach Rd., Rock Island, 931/837-4770, https://tnstateparks.com), **Old Stone Fort State Archaeological Park** (732 Stone Fort Dr., Manchester, 931/461-7676, https://tnstateparks.com), and **Frozen Head State Park** (964 Flat Fork Rd., Wartrace, 423/346-3318, https://tnstateparks.com) are other great choices for seeing multiple waterfalls in one spot—Old Stone Fork has a whopping 10 of them.

For something more immersive (pun intended), you can visit **The Walls of Jericho** (615/781-6622, www.tn.gov/environment), on the Tennessee-Alabama border, as part of a backpacking trip. You'll hike into and through this steep canyon, explore the pretty 30-foot waterfalls, swim, then camp overnight.

Connect with...

37 Lace up your boots for an urban hike
42 Dig deep in a Tennessee cave

42 Dig deep in a Tennessee cave

Outdoor Adventures • Day Trips

Why Go: Tennessee's many caves are home to music venues, underground lakes, waterfalls, and cave art.

Where: There are opportunities to go underground in much of the state, but the caves listed here are in Middle Tennessee (around Nashville) and the Cumberland Plateau (the eastern highlands).

Timing: Some caves only offer tours in high tourist season, while others have special events for holidays like Halloween and Christmas.

Beneath Tennessee's soil are more than 10,000 known caves, carved by underground streams and rivers over thousands of years. Visit the state's most popular caves on a guided group tour, where you can walk, crawl, and scoot your way through an underground ecosystem.

Many caves are parts of larger cavern systems, which means there are a variety of routes and tours available. Some cave tours are BYOF (bring your own flashlight), while others provide headlamps or lanterns. They may require shimmying through narrow passages and stooping to allow for low overhead clearance. For the most part, though, Tennessee's caves have been adapted so that everyone can enjoy them (okay, maybe not people with claustrophobia). Some have accessible entrances and are used as music venues, campgrounds, and church sanctuaries. Some are protected archaeological sites, and others house springs, whose water feeds the state's renowned whiskey distilleries.

Wear sturdy, closed-toe shoes with good traction. The temperature in a cave is usually 56-59°F, so bring a warm layer, even in summer. Prepare to hear fascinating tales, narrated by rangers who know exactly where to find cave drawings, stalactites, and waterfalls. (You're also sure to hear some cheesy cave-themed jokes.)

With its large entrance and great natural acoustics, **The Caverns** (555 Charlie Roberts Rd., Pelham, 931/516-9724, www.thecaverns.com) is an ideal venue for the subterranean concerts that are held several times per week. The underground venue can accommodate up to

Dunbar Cave State Park

view from inside Dunbar Cave

The Lost Sea

1,200 people, and tickets often sell out. This is where PBS's *Bluegrass Underground* series is now recorded. The caves, which are about 90 minutes southeast of Nashville, near Monteagle and Sewanee, are open daily for tours. You'll walk under stalactites and see an underground room that's larger than the size of three football fields.

Perhaps the greatest tourist draw in the Cumberland Plateau is **Cumberland Caverns** (1437 Cumberland Caverns Rd., McMinnville, 931/668-4396, http://cumberlandcaverns.com), a cave system with an underground ballroom, plus stalactites and stalagmites, waterfalls and pools, and a historic saltpeter mine. The ballroom's quarter-ton crystal chandelier isn't a gift of nature, but the acoustics are, so the space is regularly used for underground concerts. Many of the cave tours are suitable for kids, but some are more strenuous. Other options include special holiday tours for Halloween and Christmas, bible-themed tours (with church services), and even overnight packages where you can sleep in the caves. Season passes are available if you get hooked.

Head 45 miles northwest of downtown Nashville to **Dunbar Cave State Park** (401 Old Dunbar Cave Rd., Clarksville, 931/648-5526, http://tnstateparks.com) to find a site of historic importance. Native Americans took shelter inside this cave as early as 10,000 years ago. Mississippian Indians (1000-1450 CE) also used the cave, leaving evidence in the form of cave art on the walls. Much later on, in the 1930s, Dunbar was a mineral bath resort. In 1948, country music megastar Roy Acuff bought the resort and broadcast a live country music show from the cave. The resort eventually closed, and the state park system took it over in 1973. Rangers will cover all of this and more on the tour, helping you interpret the cave drawings (like the one that appears to be a comet flying through the sky) and pointing out a few structures left over from the resort.

Nearly three hours from downtown Nashville and a little more than an hour from Chattanooga and Knoxville, **The Lost Sea** (140 Lost Sea Rd., Sweetwater, 423/337-6616, http://the-lostsea.com) is exactly what it sounds like: a four-acre underground lake in Craighead Cavern. It's the largest underground lake in the northern hemisphere. On a glass-bottomed boat tour through the clear water, you'll see some rock formations as you learn about the cave's history, from early Native American residents to saltpeter mining operations during the Civil War.

Chattanooga's Lookout Mountain is home to **Ruby Falls** (1720 S. Scenic Hwy., Chatta-

Local Lore

In the early 1800s, the legend goes, a woman named Kate Betts believed she was cheated in a land deal by her neighbor John Bell. She vowed to haunt him, and his descendants, from then on. The tales of sights of the Bell Witch were so spooky that even then-General Andrew Jackson didn't want to stay on Bell Farm. The farm is no longer standing, but you can experience the scary stuff yourself at the **Bell Witch Cave** (430 Keysburg Rd., Adams, 615/696-3055, http://bellwitchcave.com), which is on that land that Kate Betts first battled for.

nooga, 423/821-2544, www.rubyfalls.com), a 145-foot waterfall deep underground. On the 1.5-hour tour, you'll walk paved paths through the cave as your guide tells silly jokes. Though the colored lights on the rock formations can feel garish, it's hard not to be impressed when you reach the spot where Ruby Falls thunders down to the pool below.

Connect with...

41 Go chasing waterfalls

44 Climb, bike, and paddle in Chattanooga

45 Go underground at Mammoth Cave

43 Escape to Monteagle and Sewanee

Weekend Getaways • Families and Kids

Why Go: Take a break from daily life by retreating to neighboring small towns high up on the Cumberland Plateau.

Where: Monteagle and Sewanee are 90 miles from Nashville and 6 miles apart from each other, atop a mountain.

Timing: Take a weekend to see both towns, which are more temperate in summer than many other Tennessee locales. Sewanee also makes a good stopover en route to Chattanooga.

Southeast of Nashville, on either side of I-24, are the mountain communities of Monteagle and Sewanee. Monteagle is home to a popular retreat and upscale restaurants. Sewanee is an elegant university town that's surrounded by nature. These adjacent towns offer a pastoral setting in which you can truly get away from it all.

Few communities in Tennessee are as surprising as Monteagle. The town is a speck on the map, mostly a collection of residential neighborhoods. But since 1882 it's been home to **Monteagle Assembly** (1 Assembly Ave., 931/924-2286, http://monteaglesundayschoolassembly. org), a retreat and oasis. Originally it was an ecumenical training center for Sunday school teachers patterned after the Chautauqua Institution in New York. Over the years, though, the Assembly has become more secular. Today, it's kind of like a wholesome summer camp for the entire family, with art classes, lectures and workshops, and musical performances. (Many of the lecture topics have a religious perspective, but others focus on local history, health and fitness, or nature and the environment.) You can rent a charming cottage on the Assembly's wooded, hilly campus or just buy a daily ticket to participate in the various activities.

Monteagle offers a few choices for upscale restaurants; one of them is even on the National Historic Register. Make a reservation to dine at **The High Point** (224 E. Main St., 931/924-4600, www.highpointrestaurant.net), which serves coconut shrimp, steaks, and truffle pota-

▲ All Saints' Chapel in Sewanee

▲ Memorial Cross

▲ overlooking the Cumberland Plateau

toes in a mansion built in 1929 by Al Capone. It's famous for its hidden escape hatches and secret storage areas where Capone hid liquor and other contraband.

Eat like a local by stopping in **Mountain Goat Market** (109 Main St., 931/924-2727, www.mtngoatmarket.com). The menu includes sandwiches (vegetarian or towering piles of meat), pizzas, and salads, plus desserts (try the cannoli and fruit tarts) and a coffee bar. The walls are painted with a fun goat mural, and a few tables and stools are set up for on-site dining. Or you can grab your sandwiches and chocolate-covered strawberries to go and save them for a post-hike picnic.

Sewanee is so synonymous with the **University of the South** (735 University Ave., 931/598-1000, http://sewanee.edu) that folks call the school by the town name. The private liberal arts college, owned by the Episcopal Church, has educated more than two dozen Rhodes scholars. Though the student population is less than 2,000, the campus occupies 13,000 acres of land (called "the domain"), only 1,000 of which are developed. The campus is truly breathtaking. Sewanee's buildings are grand, evoking old European castles. The modern buildings are

▲ Sewanee campus

Local Lore

Several sights on the University of the South's campus are said to be haunted, including **All Saints' Chapel.** It's said that the Perambulating Professor is the ghost of a faculty member from the school's early days who roams school paths in his slippers. Annie Armour, the author of the book *Haunted Sewanee,* estimates there are more than 70 haunted spots around campus.

carefully constructed to blend in with the older ones, giving the campus a planned, uniform appeal.

For a dramatic view over the western part of the Cumberland Plateau, drive to an **overlook** at the end of Tennessee Avenue, past the School of Theology. At the site is the striking **Memorial Cross.** It's particularly picturesque at sunrise and sunset, and there's a roundabout with parking for taking in the view.

Part of **South Cumberland State Park** (931/924-2980, https://tnstateparks.com), the **Sewanee Natural Bridge** is 25 feet tall and spans 50 feet. The naturally formed arch is set among trees and other rocks, and it's possible to cross over it on foot, as well as admire it from below. Reach it via a short footpath from the parking area. Take care as you walk over and around this natural wonder. The bridge is about four miles out of town. Drive west along Highway 41, then turn left onto Highway 56 and follow the signs.

Traffic can be tough in this area. Drivers on I-24 struggle with the winding mountain road. (Johnny Cash even sang "Monteagle Mountain" about it.) Keep your eyes on the road. Cell service can be spotty, which is ideal for unplugging, but not as great if you get lost. Pack a paper map or atlas when you set out.

Take a weekend to disconnect from everyday life in Monteagle and Sewanee. It's an ideal way to appreciate the charms of small-town Tennessee as well as the natural beauty of the Cumberland Plateau.

Connect with...

44 Climb, bike, and paddle in Chattanooga

44 Climb, bike, and paddle in Chattanooga

Outdoor Adventures • Weekend Getaways

Why Go: On the banks of the Tennessee River, in between the Cumberland Plateau and the Appalachian Mountains, charming Chattanooga is surrounded by nature's finest recreational opportunities.

Where: 130 miles southeast of downtown Nashville • www.visitchattanooga.com

Timing: The city sparkles brightest in fall, when vivid foliage reflects in the water and the temperature is comfortably warm. It's also when the most interesting events take place, like the **3 Sisters Bluegrass Festival, RiverRocks Chattanooga,** a celebration of all things outdoor, and **Chattajack,** a major stand-up paddleboarding race. Plan to spend at least two days here.

Outdoor recreation is Chattanooga's lifeblood. Within just a few minutes of downtown you can be rock climbing, hiking, biking, or paddling. There are also museums, shops, and restaurants, of course, but that's where people go *after* they get off the mountain or the river.

To get a firsthand understanding of Chattanooga's natural offerings, start by going up. One of the two main peaks here, **Lookout Mountain** (www.lookoutmountain.com) straddles the Tennessee and Georgia border. The snaky drive up takes about 15 minutes from downtown. Along the way, you can stop at popular tourist attractions **Ruby Falls** (1720 S. Scenic Hwy., 423/821-2544, www.rubyfalls.com), a thundering waterfall inside a cave, and **Rock City** (1400 Patten Rd., 706/820-2531, www.seerockcity.com), a hokey rock garden that boasts an impressive view of seven states.

From there head a couple miles north to **Point Park** (110 Point Park Rd., www.nps.gov/chch), part of Chickamauga & Chattanooga National Military Park. Point Park overlooks the Cumberland Plateau, Chattanooga, and the Cherokee National Forest. The flat, manicured paths (with a few staircases) make for an easy walk with picturesque views of the winding Tennessee River. Next, head about a mile south to **Sunset Rock** (314 W. Brow Rd.) for a short, steep hike that leads to striking vistas and a route for experienced rock climbers.

1: Sunset Rock on Lookout Mountain **2:** West Village **3:** Julia Falls Overlook **4:** Point Park

About a 20-minute drive north of downtown is the area's other peak, **Signal Mountain.** Named because it's thought that Cherokee people once lit signal fires from its peak, the mountain is now the site of an upscale residential community of the same name. There are fewer tourist attractions here than at Lookout, but no shortage of views or hikes.

A top hiking spot is on the west side, at **Signal Point** (part of Chickamauga & Chattanooga National Military Park, www.nps.gov/chch). From the wheelchair- and stroller-accessible **Julia Falls Overlook** on the **Cumberland Trail,** you can look out at the scenic Tennessee River Gorge. If you're up for a more challenging and technical hike, continue northeast on the trail for about a mile to check out misty **Rainbow Falls** as it plunges into a pretty lake. From Signal Point you can also trek to **Edward's Point** for more views of the gorge. This is a strenuous 5.8-mile (round-trip) route.

Chattanooga's outdoor charms aren't just land-based. Don't miss the opportunity to paddleboard or kayak right downtown on the Tennessee River. Rent gear from **Chattanooga Paddleboards** (111 Frazier Ave., 423/702-1422, www.chattanoogapaddleboards.com) or **L2 Outside** (100 Market St., 423/531-7873, http://l2outside.com). Canoers should head to **Chattanooga Nature Center** (400 Garden Rd., 423/821-1160, www.reflectionriding.org), where you can get out on **Lookout Creek.** Nearby **Nickajack Lake** (1265 Hales Bar Rd.) is popular with anglers and boaters. If you're an experienced paddler, it's possible to follow the 31-mile route from downtown to the lake. (Expect to battle winds in the gorge.) The city's launch areas are well-designed for paddlers, with railings to assist in sliding boats down staircases.

Riding a bike is a great, low-impact way to see the city. **Bike Chattanooga** (http://bike-chattanooga.com) offers 42 bike rental stations throughout the city. Go along the riverfront and across the bright blue **Walnut Street Bridge** (1 Walnut St.). It's almost a half-mile long, making it one of the longest pedestrian bridges in the country. From this popular spot you'll have views of the Tennessee River, the city's architecture, and the surrounding bluffs.

As darkness falls, put your gear away and explore the city's other appeals. In two cozy neighborhoods, where live music is performed on various street corners, you'll find a concentration of restaurants, bars, and hotels. Adorned with twinkling lights, the **West Village** is dotted with small businesses. At **Easy Bistro & Bar** (801 Chestnut St., 423/266-1121, www.easybistro.com), award-winning chefs create French-inspired dishes. There's also a raw bar

Local Lore

In 1941 the Glenn Miller Orchestra recorded the song "Chattanooga Choo Choo" about the city's railroad station, making it a popular destination. The station eventually fell into disrepair but was restored in the 1970s. Today, the Beaux Arts-style building houses a hotel, a music venue, a museum, shops, and restaurants.

and an impressive cocktail list. The **Station Street** area features the train-themed **Chattanooga Choo Choo Hotel** (1400 Market St., 423/266-5000, www.choochoo.com), along with art galleries, chocolate shops, and a distillery.

After all of that, you'll want to rest up for another day of activity. The West Village's **Bode Chattanooga** (730 Chestnut St., 844/431-2633, www.bode.co) has apartment-style hotel rooms with high ceilings, kitchens, and bike storage.

Connect with...

43 Escape to Monteagle and Sewanee

52 Get soaked whitewater rafting on the Ocoee River

45 Go underground at Mammoth Cave

Mammoth Cave National Park, Kentucky

Outdoor Adventures • Families and Kids • Day Trips

Why Go: The largest cave system in the world is in Kentucky, less than an hour and a half from downtown Nashville. Plan a day trip or a camping weekend to immerse yourself in this underground world.

Where: 87 miles northeast of downtown • Mammoth Cave Visitor Center, Mammoth Cave, KY • 270/758-2180, www.nps.gov/maca • free admission, tours $6-60

Timing: There are more tours offered in summer—both in frequency and type—but there are more crowds, too, so book your tickets a few weeks in advance. The temperature is consistently 54°F inside the caves, regardless of season, so bring layers.

If you've rolled your eyes on hokey cave tours before—the kinds with flashing lights and jokes about stalactites—you're in for something different when you get to Mammoth Cave National Park. The cave system here is massive: More than 400 miles have been charted so far, and new passages are being uncovered all the time. To explore the park's offerings, you'll need to take an official tour led by a park ranger; expect a deep dive into geology and history (with, yes, the occasional cave pun).

Depending on the time of year, there may be more than a dozen options of different cave tours, each with a different theme, route, level of exertion, and duration. The **Violet City Lantern Tour** is my favorite because it gives me a sense of what it would have been like to encounter the caves more than a century ago, back before flashlights and electric lights. (Of course, they didn't have maps, park rangers, or emergency exits either—but I'm glad for these anachronistic safety measures!). A ranger hands you a lantern that casts a warm glow on the nooks and crannies of the caves. You'll see the soot lines left from decades of lantern explorers, and where they wrote their names on the cave walls (that's no longer allowed). I love watching the line of lanterns of my fellow cave-goers snaking like a luminaria through the cave as I hear about its history. It is otherworldly, but not scary. To take the Violet City tour, children must be older than six (old enough to carry a lantern and hike at the same time, I suppose).

Mammoth Cave National Park

stalactites in Mammoth Cave

inside the cave

stairs leading to Mammoth Cave

On the tours, you'll learn about the Native Americans who first discovered these underground labyrinths between 5,000 to 2,000 BCE. Mammoth Cave is on Shawandasse Tula (Shawanwaki/Shawnee) and S'atsoyaha (Yuchi) land. Rangers will walk you through the myriad of purposes these caves have served over the years, including a mine for minerals like saltpeter, a site for church services, and a home for ill-fated tuberculosis treatments. Rangers aren't shy about pointing out the ways that centuries of explorers, scientists, musicians, and developers both preserved the land and abused it.

The tours follow different routes and don't necessarily overlap, so I like to take more than one during a visit. The **Domes and Dripstones Tour** is focused on the stalagmites and stalactites and the geology of the underground maze, so it is a nice balance to the history of the Violet City tour. Plus, kids of all ages are welcome. You can do them back-to-back, or take a weekend and do one a day, enjoying above-ground frolicking and camping under the stars afterward.

As its name suggests, Mammoth Cave National Park is focused on underground attractions—80 percent of the people who come to the park take cave tours. But the above-ground

▲ Mammoth Cave National Park

Cool Creatures

Inside the caves, there's no natural light—a pitch blackness that humans rarely get to experience. The local residents, such as the endangered eyeless fish, eyeless cave shrimp, and cave crickets, have adapted to the lack of light. You may need a flashlight or lantern, but they don't need no stinkin' eyeballs to know what's going on.

recreation shouldn't be ignored. There are almost 85 miles of trails designed for horseback riders, hikers, and mountain bikers. They wind their way up and down steep hills and along flat expanses—there are some wheelchair-accessible trails, too. They lead to sinkholes, to meadows filled with wildflowers (such as Eggert's sunflower, which was once an endangered species but has now recovered), and to the historic **Old Guides' Cemetery.** The cemetery includes the grave of Stephen Bishop, an enslaved man who is credited with exploring and discovering many of the most popular parts of the cave.

Bring closed-toe shoes and a jacket for walking in the caves, but pack a swimsuit and sunscreen, too, so you can kayak, paddleboard, or canoe on the Green or Nolin Rivers, both of which run through the park. Their dam-fed waters are typically between 72-75°F, which is a welcome refreshing cool-off from the heat of a Kentucky summer. There are outfitters, including **Cave Country Canoe** (856 Old Mammoth Cave Rd., Cave City, 270/773-5552, www.cavecountrycanoeky.com), who serve the area and will rent you boats and shuttle you back if you don't have your own gear.

Connect with...
42 Dig deep in a Tennessee cave

46 Drive the Natchez Trace Parkway

Outdoor Adventures • Scenic Drives • Day Trips

Why Go: Drive, bike, or walk in the footsteps of Native Americans, Kaintuck boatmen, preservationists, and others who carved out and immortalized this route.

Where: 17 miles southwest of Nashville; northern terminus crosses Highway 100 • 800/305-7417, http://nps.gov/natr • 24 hours daily • free

Timing: This is a trip you can do year-round, with wildflowers blooming in the spring, waterfalls roaring in the summer, leaves changing color in the fall, and wide-open vistas in the winter.

How long you spend on the Trace is up to you. With a full day, you can explore the 100-plus miles of the parkway that lie within Tennessee. While it's possible to drive the entire length of the Trace in one day, I don't recommend it. Take a week or more; if ever a place were about the journey and not the destination, it's the Natchez Trace.

I don't know how many times I've driven the Natchez Trace Parkway. I've lost count. But never once in all those times have I gotten bored. So, when I was talking to a woman years ago about the Trace and she said she found the route boring, I was aghast. *Boring?* I wanted to shout, "Is hiking boring? Is biking in an idyllic setting boring? Are sunsets uninterrupted by city lights boring?"

Not everywhere is for everyone, of course. But even now, years later, I still can't imagine that such a singular place would ever conjure up the B-word. Being on the Trace's winding route is far from boring—it's like hearing a meandering and epic tale, chock-full of lore.

The Natchez Trace Parkway is 444 miles long, stretching from Nashville to Natchez, Mississippi. It's a historic route with no billboards or commercial structures, just miles of curving road, verdant meadows, and crashing waterfalls. The two-lane parkway follows a path that's 10,000 years old, originally trod by buffalo who made their way back and forth to water sources. The first humans to travel what is now considered the Natchez Trace were probably Choctaw and Chickasaw people, making the first footpaths through the region. Early European settlers recognized the importance of this land route; the Trace became an official post road linking

riders on the Natchez Trace Parkway

⊿ Double Arch Bridge

Nashville and Natchez in 1801. By 1820, more than 20 inns, referred to as "stands," were open, serving the diverse array of people who traveled the Trace. In 1909, the Daughters of the American Revolution in Mississippi started a project to preserve the Trace, which had by then been rendered obsolete by steamboats, railways, and better roads. It wasn't until 2005 that the route was fully protected and restored.

Today, each mile of the Trace is clearly marked, and the route is speckled with historically significant spots marked by turnouts and informational signage. Perhaps the most photographed stop is the striking **Double Arch Bridge** (milepost 438), the first bridge in the country to be built from segments of concrete. You can see it from above, at **Birdsong Hollow,** with views overlooking Franklin's pastoral scenery, and from ground level, where the bridge's arches look especially dramatic. If you have limited time, a quick drive from Nashville to the bridge is worthwhile. I'm also a fan of the **Baker Bluff Overlook** (milepost 405.1). Sunset at Baker Bluff is marked by pink skies rising over the farmland below. This overlook connects with hiking trails, so it can be as active or relaxing a stop as you like.

Local Lore

The land near milepost 390.7 was once so rich in limestone phosphate that the area was known as the Phosphate Capital of the World. At this spot on the Trace, you can take a short walk (0.2-mile round-trip) to get a glimpse of what remains of a 19th-century phosphate mining town called **Gordonsburg.** Look for the old mine shaft and the foliage that has grown over the limestone. The sunken path you're walking on is an abandoned railroad route, used to transport the phosphate.

There are even a few places where you can pull over and walk (and in one case, drive) sections of the **original Trace.** These sunken, unpaved indentations, often blanketed by leaves, are striking reminders of the thousands of people and horses that used this road before there were interstates, steamboats, or airplanes. At these spots, I can't help but feel awe for the people who traveled such massive distances on foot.

The National Park Service maintains three **campgrounds** along the Trace, plus five bicyclist-only campsites with more modest amenities. The northernmost bike campsite is located at the intersection of the Trace and Highway 50, about 36 miles south of Nashville.

Most of the Trace's stops have picnic tables and shade. A few have restrooms and other amenities. The Trace's speed limit is 50 mph. Cars are required to give cyclists the right of way. When you're driving on the parkway, give cyclists plenty of room by moving into the opposite lane if it's safe to do so.

For more detailed information on the Trace, check out my book, *Moon Nashville to New Orleans Road Trip.* It covers all 444 miles of the parkway, along with detours and side trips. The National Park Service publishes a foldout map and guide to the parkway, too.

Connect with...

47 Meet makers and mules in Columbia

49 Better understand the Civil War in Corinth, Mississippi

47 Meet makers and mules in Columbia

Art and Culture • Day Trips

Why Go: Charming small-town vibes, a groovy maker culture, and a thing for mules make Columbia a must-do day trip.

Where: Columbia is 45 miles—about an hour's drive—from downtown Nashville.

Timing: Columbia's First Fridays, the monthly evening event that invites you to stroll among the galleries and shops, is a reliably magical night of food trucks, pink-hued skies, live music, and bargain buys.

The thing you need to know about Columbia, Tennessee, is that this small town has long had an affinity for mules that borders on obsession. It's rooted in the weekly mule markets that took place here in the 19th and early 20th centuries, a time when work animals were indispensable to Tennessee farmers. In many cases, mules were a farmer's most valuable asset—a good pair of mules could make a poor farmer rich. The animals were more expensive and highly prized than horses or oxen because they were said to be stronger, smarter, and more surefooted than other work animals.

At the time, Columbia hosted a yearly mule market, which opened on the first Monday of April. People flocked here to buy and sell the animals. Other nearby towns, including Lynchburg and Paris, were also known for large mule sales, but Columbia, then called the mule capital of the world, hosted the biggest market of them all.

Visiting Columbia today, you're more likely to see a painting of a mule than the real thing, but the town still holds the animals in high regard. As an homage to the mule markets of the past, Columbia celebrates **Mule Day** every year during the first week of April. (Yes, it's called "Mule *Day*," but events actually take place over six days). Mule Day is a festival of music, crafts, and food, all in celebration of the mule. You likely won't buy a mule here—although you can—but you will learn about the hard-working animal, and you can buy almost any piece of art or clothing—or pottery, or cookie—emblazoned with its image.

W7thCo Gallery

The rest of the year, Columbia is a quiet but thriving small town with an active art scene. In the 2010s, affordable real estate, particularly warehouses, lead to an influx of artists and makers, who converted these spaces into studios and galleries. One centerpiece of the activity is the **Columbia Arts Building** (307 W. 11th St., 931/334-0036, www.columbiaartsbuilding. com), a hub for artists who want to work in a collaborative environment. Much of the space is open to the public, so you can browse or see artists at work. The creative energy is palpable. CAB, as it's called, also has a juice shop/café and an outdoor dining area that's perfect for feasting on items from the food trucks that often stop here.

A few blocks to the northeast, downtown Columbia is arranged around a public square, with small, locally owned retail businesses encircling the picturesque Maury County government building. Adjacent to the square is the one-of-a-kind **W7thCo Gallery** (107 W. 7th St., 931/446-1900, https://gallery.w7thco.com), where you can get a visual education on Columbia's past. The gallery displays and sells historic photographs of the town. Notably, all of the photos are printed from salvaged negatives from Orman Studio, a photography studio that operated in Columbia from the 1930s to 2011. Exhibits change monthly, usually on a theme, from Columbia's famed mule sales to its surfeit of car dealerships in the 1940s. There's something moving about seeing these historic images printed with modern technology in a contemporary gallery. Other downtown shops include **Ted's Sporting Goods** (806 S. Main St., 931/388-6387, www.tedssportinggoods.com), with its upside-down sign, **Duck River Books** (12 Public Sq., 931/548-2665, https://duckriverbooks.com), and **Variety Records** (24 Public Sq., 931/982-6212).

North of downtown is **New South Marketplace** (510 N. Garden St.), a collection of shops with artistic themes, including **Needle and Grain** (931/548-6686, https://needle-andgrain.com), which stocks local crafts, gifts, and home goods, and **Muletown Pottery** (931/626-1195), which sells local ceramics, but also lets you make your own pottery. On First Friday nights, New South stays open late and hosts a food truck plaza, with many dining options to choose from, plus live music, transforming the parking lot into a magical party. You may head here for the mules, but you'll stay for the makers (and the meals).

Reassessing History

In 1850, Columbia was the third-largest city in Tennessee (behind Nashville and Memphis), a wealthy place that profited off the enslaved Black people who were forced to work on plantations in the area. The economic impacts of the Civil War-ravaged Columbia were significant, and in the century that followed, the town struggled.

In 1946, the city was the site of racially motivated violence, in which a white mob attacked the town's Black community in a neighborhood known as Mink Slide. More than 100 Black men and women were arrested; none of the white instigators were charged with a crime. A legal team comprised of future Supreme Court Justice Thurgood Marshall and two local attorneys, Z. Alexander Looby and Maurice Weaver, would eventually help 24 of the 25 Black defendants gain an acquittal. (The 25th defendant received a reduced sentence.)

Today, Columbia is working on telling this shameful history in a complete and honest manner. Efforts are underway to preserve the **A. J. Morton Funeral Home** (115 E. 8th St.), where Black residents gathered during the violent events in 1946. It currently has a historic marker out front, which gives an overview of the events and outcome of the trials. **Visit Columbia** (713 N. Main St., www.visitcolumbiatn.com), the city's tourism bureau, offers several self-guided driving tours, including one on the area's African American history, which notes homes and businesses that free Black people owned and operated during the Civil War and Reconstruction, as well as some of the landmarks of Mink Slide.

Connect with...

46 Drive the Natchez Trace Parkway

48 Trace the origins of country music to Bristol

Art and Culture • Weekend Getaways

Why Go: This is the birthplace of country music. Everything you love about country can be traced back to Bristol.

Where: 300 miles northeast of downtown Nashville • http://discoverbristol.org

Timing: A long weekend is enough time to immerse yourself in Bristol's charms. September brings cool temperatures and vivid foliage, as well as the **Bristol Rhythm & Roots Reunion,** a three-day, city-wide festival of live music. The Bristol Motor Speedway draws more than 150,000 people on major race days, so check ahead if you want to attend a race—or avoid the crowds.

In 1927, a talent scout named Ralph Peer came to Bristol, Tennessee, to record local musicians. Peer chose Bristol as his destination because it was the largest urban center in the Appalachian region. Peer's advertisements in the newspaper initially generated a limited response, but when news emerged that artists were being paid up to $100 in cash on the spot and could earn more in royalties, Peer had to schedule night sessions to accommodate everyone.

During these now-famous "Bristol Sessions," Peer recorded the Carter Family and Jimmie Rodgers. Virtually overnight, both became commercial successes. Today they're credited as the first popular country music stars. Musicologists note that Peer made little attempt to coach or influence the artists who came to record, so the sessions are an accurate portrayal of the music of the period. In addition, the business model that Peer established, where performers were paid cash up front for recording and then earned royalties for each record sold, formed the basis of the modern recording industry.

Record labels continued to schedule field sessions around Tennessee in the succeeding years, hoping to replicate the success of Bristol in 1927. The Great Depression and other economic and social forces put an end to field sessions by the early 1930s. But the genre that had been born in Bristol was established, and music has never been the same. In 1998, Congress declared Bristol the birthplace of country music.

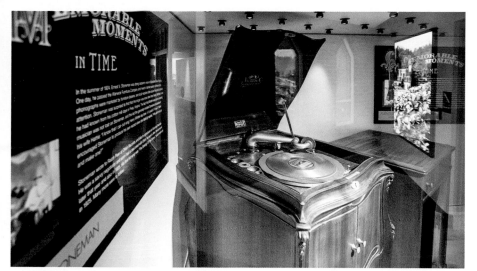

▲ exhibit at the Birthplace of Country Music Museum

▲ Birthplace of Country Music Museum

Set in a glass-and-brick building, the **Birthplace of Country Music Museum** (101 Country Music Way, 423/573-1927, www.birthplaceofcountrymusic.org) is a repository of the early days of country music and all that it begat. The collection includes microphones, sheet music, posters, recordings, and much more. The museum also has a rotating special exhibit that changes two or three times a year; past exhibits focused on Cecil Sharp, the Carter Family, and American roots music. Radio Bristol, a non-profit community station, broadcasts from the museum, producing a number of live events. The nationally syndicated *Farm and Fun Time* variety show, both a throwback to days gone by and a modern take on today's country music, is particularly entertaining.

After taking in the museum, wander downtown Bristol. **State Street** is a pleasant row of charming retail shops, with a few restaurants and bars along the way. Notably, one side of the street is in Tennessee, while the other is in Virginia. One of the city's most famous landmarks is the **Bristol VA-TENN Sign** (State St. at 3rd St.), which spans the eastern end of the street. Driving down the street headed east, it's fun to watch the sign, declaring Bristol "A Good Place

▲ Bristol Rhythm & Roots Reunion

to Live," come into focus as you approach. But this isn't the only gold mine of a photo op in Bristol. Perhaps you've seen the commercial with Geico's animated gecko standing on State Street. Feel free to mimic him with your own state-straddling pic; just watch for cars.

After your selfies, head to **Tennessee Ernie Ford's home** (1223 Anderson St., 276/466-9116, http://bristolhistoricalassociation.com). Bristol native Ernest Jennings Ford was a country and gospel star during the 1950s and '60s. The small home is stocked with artifacts from Ford's life as well as early-20th-century country music memorabilia. Whether you stop by just to see the outside, or take the tour (by appointment), remember to bless everyone's pea-pickin' hearts, just like Ernie always did.

Other highlights of downtown include the **L.C. King Factory Store** (24 7th St., 423/764-5188, http://lcking.com), which sells ready-for-the-elements clothing and offers tours of its factory. **Blackbird Bakery** (56 Piedmont Ave., 276/645-5754, http://blackbirdbakerybristol.com) is open 24 hours, six days a week for coffee, pastries, and desserts, plus live music in the evenings. (It's closed on Sundays.)

Bristol has two hotels downtown, making it easy to spend the weekend immersing yourself here. The **Bristol Hotel** (510 Birthplace of Country Music Way, 276/696-3535, www.bristolhotelva.com) is right next door to the Birthplace of Country Music Museum. **Sessions Hotels** (833 State St., 276/285-5040, www.sessionshotel.com) is housed in a former candy factory and grain mill, with lots of historic detailing in the rooms.

Connect with...

30 Get deep into country music at the Hall of Fame

49

Better understand the Civil War

in Corinth, Mississippi

Weekend Getaways

Why Go: Corinth is chock-full of Civil War history, offering a breadth and depth of information that might surprise you. The old-fashioned soda fountain and boutique-laden downtown is the cherry on top.

Where: 170 miles southwest of downtown • Corinth Area Convention and Visitors Bureau, 215 N. Fillmore St., 662/287-8300, www.corinth.net

Timing: Many shops and restaurants are closed on Sundays. If you visit on a weekend, check out the battlefield site in Shiloh on Sunday, leaving Saturday for eating, drinking, and shopping in Corinth. Try to plan your trip so you're here for at least one weekday to get the most out of Corinth. April 6-7 is the anniversary of the Battle of Shiloh, so plan to come then if you like Civil War reenactments (and crowds).

A crossroads for major transport lines, Corinth, Mississippi, was once the place where the Mobile & Ohio and Memphis & Charleston railroads met. It was a crucial hub in the Civil War; capturing the city meant access to the rail line. Nearby Shiloh, Tennessee, was essential for controlling the Tennessee River, a key waterway.

The Battle of Shiloh took place April 6-7, 1862, and was, at that point, the bloodiest battle in U.S. history, with more than 23,000 soldiers killed or wounded. Two battles in Corinth followed, on May 30 (sometimes referred to as the Siege of Corinth), and October 3-4, 1862. Union and Confederate troops battled at these sites until the Union army won control in October 1862. Today, both Shiloh and Corinth offer insights into the events and repercussions surrounding the battles.

Near the crossroads in downtown Corinth, the 15,000-square-foot **Corinth Civil War Interpretive Center** (501 W. Linden St., 662/287-9273, www.nps.gov/shil) is the best place to start learning more about the battles. Here, you'll examine maps and dioramas that show the chronology of the battles, and you can watch films that detail the soldiers' experiences. Outside the center is a water feature called *The Stream of American History*. The water's source is a fountain in which a large stone tablet depicts the Preamble to the United States Constitution.

1: Abe's Grill **2:** Corinth Contraband Camp
3: Verandah-Curlee House **4:** Shiloh Military
Park

The water flows in a path that gradually widens until it reaches a haphazard pile of stone blocks that represent significant battles of the Civil War. The blocks vary in size, representing the number of people killed in each battle. It's a quiet, reflective place.

Next, take the 20-minute drive to the **Shiloh Battlefield Visitor Center at Shiloh Military Park** (1055 Pittsburg Landing Rd., Shiloh, 731/689-5696, www.nps.gov/shil). Start with the center's 32-minute film, which gives a detailed overview of the battle that took place here and the role that the surrounding topography played. From the visitors center, continue to the battlefield. Here, color-coded signs show the positions of the Union and Confederate armies. As you stand where the markers are, you can look out and see the rolling hills and valleys that the soldiers traversed.

Most people see the park on a self-guided driving tour. The route takes you by a replica of the log **Shiloh Church,** which was destroyed by Union troops, and to the **Shiloh National Cemetery,** which holds more than 3,500 graves of Civil War soldiers. Don't miss the view of the Tennessee River from the bluff at the cemetery. The tour offers more than just military history: At the **Shiloh Indian Mounds Site,** you can see remains from a Woodland-period (1000 CE) Indigenous village. The six green mounds with flat tops were likely buildings, while the rounded mound is likely a burial site.

Back in Corinth proper, the powerful **Corinth Contraband Camp** (800 N. Parkway St., Corinth, 662/287-9273, www.nps.gov/shil) is where escaped enslaved people sought safety behind Union lines. The camp became a profitable cooperative farm, providing a first step to freedom for workers. From its founding in 1862 until December 1863, when the camp was relocated to Memphis, more than 6,000 freed Black people, including children, lived and worked here. Today, the site is an open, leafy sculpture park. Along a short walkway, you can admire bronze sculptures and read about the kinds of jobs the people here had, and the profits they made as a community. Download the park's smartphone app to learn more about the camp.

Corinth offers a fast-paced way to check out its other charms with the self-guided **60 Sights in 60 Minutes walking tour.** Grab a brochure from the Corinth CVB or download the smartphone app from the town's website and embark on a tour of the city's historic sites, attractions, and antiques stores. Highlights include the **Verandah-Curlee House** (705 Jackson St., 662/287-9501, https://verandahcurleehouse.com), which served as headquarters for both

Local Lore

During the Depression, Southerners, looking to stretch the little bit of fresh meat they had, added potato flour to their ground meat and called the creation a slugburger. (The name comes from the slang term for a nickel.) In Corinth, you can try one of these famous, frugal burgers for yourself at **Borroums Drug Store** (604 E. Waldron St., 662/286-3361), the oldest drugstore in continuous operation in Mississippi. Wash it down with a shake from the classic soda fountain.

Confederate and Union generals during the war, and the **Corinth Coca-Cola Museum** (601 Washington St., 662/415-7998, www.corinthcoke.com/museum), a tiny but mighty collection of all things related to the ever-popular soda. The tour also takes you past cute boutiques on Wick Street.

The other appeal of Corinth is its food. If you're here on a weekday, sit at the counter for breakfast (served 'til 3pm) at **Abe's Grill** (803 US-72 W., 662/286-6124). Do *not* skip the biscuits. As you dine, you'll no doubt hear a lot of stories about Corinth through the years. Though you're far north of the Mississippi Delta, you can get a fix of the region's famed tamales at **Dillworth's Tamales** (702 Wick St., 662/223-3296). Delta tamales are notably spicier than the Mexican variety, and they're sold by the sackful. Follow it all with the day's special cupcake from **Lauren's Cake Shop** (103 Taylor St., 662/415-7961). Her frosting-to-cake ratio is spot-on.

Connect with...

46 Drive the Natchez Trace Parkway

50 Witness the mountain magic of the Smokies

Great Smoky Mountains National Park

Outdoor Adventures • Weekend Getaways • Scenic Drives

Why Go: Hike and drive to incredible spots. When you see the mist draped over the mountains, you'll understand how the Smokies got their name.

Where: 215 miles from downtown Nashville, minimum 4-hour drive • Great Smoky Mountains National Park, 865/436-1200, www.nps.gov/grsm; 24 hours daily year-round; free

Timing: Autumn draws thousands of people to the park to see fall foliage. The weather is generally cool and crisp, great for hiking. In early June this is one of the few places in the country where synchronous fireflies can be seen. For a chance to see them, enter the competitive lottery on the park website. Spring is lovely, with blooming rhododendron and dogwoods—and fewer people. The weather can be less predictable, so check forecasts and pack rain gear.

The Great Smoky Mountains, a subrange of the Appalachians, are a kaleidoscope of natural features: tall peaks, babbling brooks, craggy rocks, and scenic meadows. The Smokies form the boundary between Tennessee and North Carolina in an unbroken chain that rises more than 5,000 feet for over 36 miles. Within the park's 800 square miles, scientists have documented some 10,000 species of plants, animals, and invertebrates, but some research suggests as many as 90,000 more live in this remarkably diverse natural wilderness.

There are more than 800 miles of hiking trails in the park, bringing you face-to-face with wildlife, waterfalls, and breathtaking viewpoints. You won't be able to do them all in a single weekend, but you've got to start somewhere, right? If this is your first visit to the Smokies, seeing **Clingmans Dome,** the highest point in the park (6,643 feet) is a must. At the summit, you can climb an observation tower that takes you up above the treetops for a stunning view. The path to the tower is paved, but it's not wheelchair-accessible due to its steepness.

From the Clingmans Dome parking area, you can venture to **Andrews Bald,** one of the Smokies' grassy highland meadows. It's a lovely, magical place, great for relaxing in the sun

Clingmans Dome

sunset in Great Smoky Mountains National Park

⏶ black bear in Cades Cove

or even playing a game of Frisbee or catch. Look for wildflowers in spring and blackberries in summer. The out-and-back hike to the bald is 1.8 miles each way on Forney Ridge Trail.

Another must-do for first-timers is the scenic drive at **Cades Cove,** a pastoral valley on the western end of the park. Traffic moves slowly along this 11-mile, one-way loop, passing historic structures and wildlife like black bears, deer, and coyotes. Plan on spending at least two hours on the drive. If you want to see Cades Cove on foot, visit on a Wednesday or Saturday morning in summer, when the roads are closed to vehicular traffic. Many of the trails in the area lead to refreshing mountain streams, ideal for wading and fishing.

The park's gateway communities in Tennessee—Gatlinburg, Cosby, Pigeon Forge, Sevierville, and Townsend—offer the necessities of life, plus some extravagances. Gatlinburg and Pigeon Forge in particular cater to tourists, with theme parks, mini golf, dinner theaters, and stores selling airbrushed t-shirts and homemade fudge. These kitschy towns aren't for everyone, but I'm fond of a few spots in **Gatlinburg.** I always stop at **The Donut Friar** (634 Park-

Community Focus

Country music icon Dolly Parton grew up in Locust Ridge, an area that's now part of the park system. A replica of her childhood home, built by one of her brothers, stands at the entrance to Dollywood, her theme park in Sevierville. Parton built Dollywood here in part so that visitors could appreciate the East Tennessee mountains that she loves. But more so, she wanted to create jobs in the community. Today, more than 4,000 people work at Dollywood, making it the largest employer in the area.

way, 865/436-7306), which is in the same shopping complex as **The Day Hiker** (634 Parkway, 877/329-4453, www.thedayhiker.com), so I can get gear for outings along with my carbs.

The area is also deeply rooted in mountain arts and crafts: Nearby is the **Arrowmont School of Arts and Crafts** (556 Parkway, 865/436-5860, www.arrowmont.org), which exhibits the works of its artists and offers workshops in weaving, pottery, and wood turning, to name just a few. I then drive through the **Great Smoky Mountains Arts and Crafts Community** (light 3A, E. Parkway/Hwy. 321 N., www.gatlinburgcrafts.com), which is home to about 100 artists who make their living selling their handicrafts.

Millions of people visit the Smokies each year. Once you've hiked the park's trails, admired the incredible landscape, and made yourself at home in the surrounding towns, you'll understand the magic of these mountains.

51 Follow in the footsteps of Civil Rights activists in Memphis

Black Heritage • Weekend Getaways

Why Go: If you want to understand the U.S. Civil Rights Movement, Memphis is the place to go. While the movement wasn't isolated to Memphis, it's here that the nation took notice.

Where: 215 miles southwest of downtown Nashville • www.memphistravel.com

Timing: In spring, magnolias and cherry trees bloom and azaleas and peonies add their riotous colors to days of blue skies and temperate weather. The city's largest annual event, **Memphis in May,** rolls many major festivals into a month-long celebration.

If you want to pick just one date that cemented Memphis's position in the annals of history, it might be February 1, 1968. On that day, Echol Cole and Robert Walker, two Black sanitation workers, died on the job. Less than two weeks later, more than 1,000 of the city's Black sanitation workers went on strike, protesting the dangerous labor conditions that led to the men's deaths. It was this strike that brought Dr. Martin Luther King Jr. to Memphis multiple times. And it was in Memphis, on April 4, 1968, where King was assassinated at the Lorraine Motel. These events would become some of the most significant of the U.S. Civil Rights Movement.

A visit to the **National Civil Rights Museum** (450 Mulberry St., 901/521-9699, www.civilrightsmuseum.org) is essential. Built on the site of the Lorraine Motel, the museum makes a thorough examination of the U.S. Civil Rights Movement, from enslavement to the present day. Exhibits display original letters, audio recordings, photos, and newspaper clippings from events including the Montgomery bus boycott, *Brown v. Board of Education,* Freedom Summer, and the march from Selma to Montgomery. Original and replica artifacts, such as the bus where Rosa Parks refused to move for a white passenger in 1955, and the cell where King wrote his famous *Letter from a Birmingham Jail,* help to illustrate the monumental importance of the movement. The exhibits also expand beyond MLK and the other activists of the 1950s and '60s, connecting their work to social justice movements of all kinds. The museum is a powerful experience; you could easily spend half a day here taking everything in.

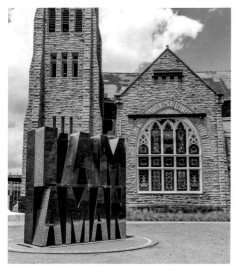

▲ Clayborn Temple

▲ Beale Street

▲ National Civil Rights Museum

There are other sites in Memphis to both learn about the movement and to pay respects to the people who championed the effort. Built in 1887, **Clayborn Temple** (294 Hernando St., https://clayborn.org) was a key gathering place and a safe haven for the protestors during the Sanitation Workers' Strike. It wasn't unusual for King to stop here when in town. The iconic "I Am a Man" signs that the sanitation strikers carried were distributed here. The church still has an active congregation today; it's also a community gathering place.

Next to the church, the **I Am a Man Plaza** was designed by Cliff Garten and John Jackson and dedicated in 2018 (the 50th anniversary of King's death). The grassy plaza bears the names of all the striking sanitation workers. Its focal point is a 12-foot-tall sculpture of the phrase, a moving remembrance that's especially beautiful when lit at night.

About a mile south is **Mason Temple Church of God in Christ** (930 Mason St., 901/947-9300, www.cogic.org), where King gave his famous "I've Been to the Mountaintop" speech. He was assassinated the next day. The temple was built in 1941, and when erected was

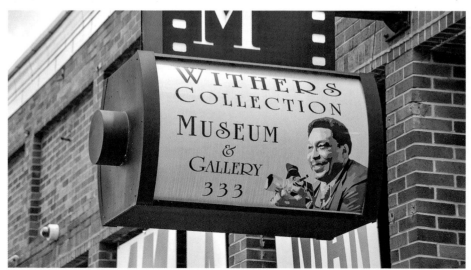

The Withers Collection Museum & Gallery

Local Lore

Memphis, on the banks of the Mississippi River, is named after the ancient Egyptian city of the same name, which stood on the banks of the Nile River. That's why you see a pyramid rising in the city's skyline, about one-tenth of its Egyptian inspiration. Over the years the pyramid has served as a sports arena and a music venue; today it's a massive sporting goods store, with a bowling alley, observation deck, restaurant, hotel, and even an indoor cypress swamp.

the largest church building owned by a predominantly Black religious denomination. It's still active today.

Photojournalist Ernest Withers documented much of the Civil Rights Movement as well as everyday life of Memphians, working for more than 60 years. See his work for yourself at **The Withers Collection Museum & Gallery** (333 Beale St., 901/523-2344, www.thewitherscollection.com). Withers' images offer a visceral insight into the fight for civil rights.

Of course, Memphis is also known as being the home of blues music. **Beale Street** is the center of the city's blues scene. No other part of Memphis has as much music and entertainment packed into such a small area. While Beale Street is more tourist-centric than it once was, it's still a worthwhile place to spend an evening, strolling from one bar to the next, stopping to listen to incredible music performances.

No trip to Memphis is complete without a good meal. Since 1946, **The Four Way** (988 Mississippi Blvd., 901/507-1519, http://fourwaymemphis.com) has been an anchor of the community, serving soul-food favorites like country-fried steak, turkey and dressing, pickled beets, and mac and cheese. King ate here when he was in town; it was also a favorite of Elvis Presley.

Connect with...

⓭ Relive the Nashville sit-ins

52

Get soaked whitewater rafting
on the Ocoee River

Outdoor Adventures • Weekend Getaways

Why Go: There's no better way to spend a day than whitewater rafting. You get the adrenaline rush from navigating the rapids, and the serenity of being out in nature.

Where: Ocoee Whitewater Center, 190 miles southeast of downtown Nashville • 3.5-hour drive

Timing: Rafting season runs March-September; June and July are the busiest months. During the summer, outfitters run daily trips. In spring and fall, trips run on weekends and holidays only. Trips are dependent on the Tennessee Valley Authority's schedule of water releases.

Chattanooga is en route to the Ocoee from Nashville, so it is an easy option for an overnight stay before or after your rafting trip.

The first time I heard a friend talk about the Ocoee River being turned off and on as we drove past an empty riverbed on our way to go rafting, I thought he was joking. But as anyone who's rafted this managed river knows, it's not a joke or hyperbole: the Tennessee Valley Authority (TVA) literally controls the flow of the Ocoee.

The TVA operates three hydroelectric dams along the 93-mile Ocoee River, which flows northwest through Tennessee. Together the dams produce some 70,000 kilowatts of electricity by diverting water from one section of the river to another. When the river water is being used to generate electricity, the Ocoee is just a trickle down an otherwise dry riverbed. But TVA releases water from the dams for recreation on certain days of the year—that's the river being "switched on." And when it's on, people from around the region come to raft and kayak the whitewater.

The Ocoee 1 dam is the farthest downstream and was built in 1910. A dozen miles upstream, Ocoee 2 was built in 1913 and consists of a diversion dam, a long wooden flume, and a powerhouse. The river's water is diverted at the site of the dam into the flume, which carries it five miles downstream to the Ocoee 2 powerhouse. From there, the water drops 250 feet, creat-

▲ whitewater rafting on the Ocoee River

▲ the Ocoee River

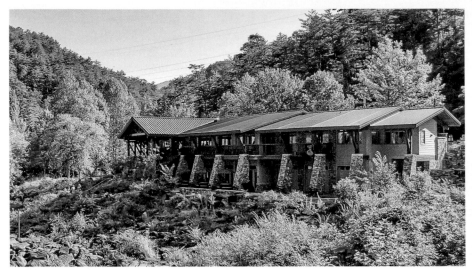

▲ Ocoee Whitewater Center

ing hydroelectric power. The line of the flume is visible as you drive along the river, resembling a trough set against the mountain. A few miles farther upstream is Ocoee 3, built in 1942. This dam holds the river's water in a reservoir.

A segment below Ocoee 2 is where the fun happens. There are more than 20 Class III-IV rapids in this four-mile stretch, which can be intimidating and dangerous if you don't know what you're doing. Fortunately, there are more than 20 licensed outfitters offering rafting trips down the Ocoee. Many trips take around 6 hours total, about 4.5 of which are on the water, but there are shorter, 3.5-hour options that spend about 2 hours on the river.

Some of the best outfitters are **Ocoee Rafting** (1548 Hwy. 68, Ducktown, 423/496-3388, www.ocoeerafting.com), **Nantahala Outdoor Center** (1680 Hwy. 64, Benton), **Ocoee Inn Rafting** (2496 Hwy. 64, Benton), and **Ocoee Adventure Center** (4651 Hwy. 64, Benton). If you want to make a more significant commitment to getting wet, you can sign up for kayaking or paddleboard whitewater clinics at NOC or OAC.

When you arrive, you'll be teamed up with a guide, usually at a ratio of six passengers and one guide per raft. You'll be issued a helmet and life jacket then get a safety briefing and instructions on how to paddle. The river alternates between calm areas and rapids, so you'll be doing a fair amount of paddling. Meanwhile, your guide will be keeping you afloat and guiding your raft safely down the river, all while keeping you entertained, pointing out the rapids' adrenaline-pumping names like Broken Nose and Double Suck.

For the trip, wear a bathing suit and rash guard (or lots of waterproof sunscreen) and shoes that will stay on your feet—no flip flops. Note that no one under 12 is permitted to raft anywhere on the Ocoee, but families with young children can have great fun on the Hiwassee or Pigeon Rivers; your outfitter will help you find the right trip for your group.

It's also possible to enjoy the Ocoee without stepping foot in a raft. The **Ocoee Whitewater Center** (4400 Hwy. 64, Ducktown, www.fs.usda.gov), near Ocoee 3, is a central source of information about the river. Run by the Forest Service, it has restrooms, rocking chairs, and good views. The two-story building is constructed entirely from materials that are local to the area. The center sits on a mile-long section of the river that was used in the 1996 Olympics. The riverbed in front of the center is pockmarked and rugged. When the water is low, children and adults will enjoy walking around the pools and streams on the riverbed or sunning on the rocks. When the water is high, this is a great place to watch rafters zooming by.

The iron-and-cable suspension **Olympic Legacy Bridge** spans the 330 feet of river in front of the center, providing nice views of the water below. During spring and summer, plan to walk through the center's Olympic gardens, which showcase native plants such as rhododendron, and feature 11 poplar trees that honor the 11 Israeli athletes who died in the 1972 Olympic Games.

Connect with...

44 Climb, bike, and paddle in Chattanooga

INDEX

PHOTO CREDITS

All photos © Margaret Littman except title page photo: Sepavo | Dreamstime.com; page 2 © (top middle) Birthplace of Country Music; (bottom middle) Courtesy of Cheekwood Estate & Gardens; (bottom) Nashville Public Library, Special Collections, Gary Layda; page 3 © (top middle) Birthplace of Country Music; (bottom middle) Courtesy of Cheekwood Estate & Gardens; (bottom) Nashville Public Library, Special Collections, Gary Layda; page 9 © Ronnie Brooks; page 10 © (top left) Nudie's Honky Tonk; (top right) Ronnie Brooks; page 11 © (top left) Swett's; page 12 © (top) Nashville Public Library, Special Collections, Gary Layda; (bottom left) Calvin L. Leake | dreamstime.com; (bottom right) Nashville Public Library, Special Collections, Gary Layda; page 13 © (top) Johnny Cash Museum / Patsy Cline Museum; (bottom) Birthplace of Country Music; page 14 © (top middle) Johnny Cash Museum / Patsy Cline Museum; (top right) Wildhorse Saloon; page 15 © (top left) Tennessee State Museum; (top right) Erik Lattwein | Dreamstime.com; page 16 © (top middle) Ronnie Brooks; (top right) Adrian Morales; page 17 © (top left) Lane Motor Museum; (top right) Game Terminal; page 18 © (top left) Pennington's Distillery; (top right) Courtesy of Cheekwood Estate & Gardens; page 20 © (top) Nashville Paddle Co.; page 21 © (top) Birthplace of Country Music; page 22 © The Listening Room; page 23 © (top) Rolf52 | dreamstime.com; (bottom) The Listening Room; page 27 © (top right) Swett's; (bottom) Swett's; page 28 © Swett's; page 31 © (top left) Signal Photos / Alamy Stock Photo; page 36 © Emily Harper Beard; page 40 © Neil Letson | dreamstime.com; page 43 © (top) Deborah Douglas; (bottom) Deborah Douglas; page 47 © (top left) Jiawangkun | Dreamstime.com; (top right) Markskalny | Dreamstime.com; (bottom) Nudie's Honky Tonk; page 51 © (top) Jessica C. Phillips; page 55 © (top right) Nathan Zucker; (bottom right) Edley's Bar-B-Que; page 57 © Edley's Bar-B-Que; page 67 © Legacy1995 | dreamstime.com; page 70 © Nashville Public Library, Special Collections, Gary Layda; page 71 © (top) Nashville Public Library, Special Collections, Gary Layda; page 75 © (top) Nashville Convention & Visitors Corp.; (bottom) Nashville Convention & Visitors Corp.; page 76 © Nashville Convention & Visitors Corp.; page 79 © (top left) Dean Dixon; (top right) Dean Dixon; (bottom) Danielle McDaniel / The Clay Lady; page 80 © Turnip Green Creative Reuse; page 83 © (bottom) Belmont University; page 87 © (top left) Ryan Green - 30mileswest; (top right) Ryan Green - 30mileswest; (bottom) The Listening Room; page 92 © courtesy of Plaza Mariachi; page 95 © Nashville Convention & Visitors Corp.; page 97 © Pennington's Distillery; page 99 © (top) Madame Tussauds Nashville; (bottom)

Madame Tussauds Nashville; page 100 © Madame Tussauds Nashville; page 103 © (top left) Game Terminal; (top right) Emily Harper Beard; (bottom) Rolf52 | Dreamstime.com; page 107 © (top right) Erik Lattwein | Dreamstime.com; page 108 © Erik Lattwein | Dreamstime.com; page 112 © Jai Mo | dreamstime.com; page 115 © (top left) Ronnie Brooks; (top right) Delgado Guitars; (bottom left) Fanny's House of Music; page 116 © Ronnie Brooks; page 119 © (top right) Thomas Lohr | dreamstime.com; page 123 © (top) Johnny Cash Museum / Patsy Cline Museum; (bottom) Johnny Cash Museum / Patsy Cline Museum; page 124 © Johnny Cash Museum / Patsy Cline Museum; page 130 © Daniel Chaney; page 133 © (bottom) Courtesy of Cheekwood Estate & Gardens; page 137 © (top) Calvin L. Leake | dreamstime.com; (bottom) Brenda Kean | dreamstime.com; page 145 © (top left) Tennessee Central Railway Museum; (top right) Lane Motor Museum; (bottom) Tennessee State Museum; page 149 © (top left) Dwong19 | dreamstime.com; page 153 © (top left) Clint Searcy; (top right) Adrian Morales; (bottom) Jessica Amerson; page 155 © Adrian Morales; page 161 © (top) Casa Azafrán; (bottom) Casa Azafrán; page 165 © (top) Schneidersimages | dreamstime.com; page 170 © Roger8777 | Dreamstime.com; page 173 © Nashville Paddle Co.; page 174 © (top) Nashville Paddle Co.; (bottom) Nashville Paddle Co.; page 177 © (bottom) Karen Foley | Dreamstime.com; page 181 © (top) Anthony Heflin | dreamstime.com; (bottom) James Vallee | dreamstime.com; page 182 © Gerald D. Tang | dreamstime.com; page 185 © (bottom) Tony Bosse | dreamstime.com; page 202 © Marek Uliasz | Dreamstime.com; page 209 © (top) Birthplace of Country Music; (bottom) Birthplace of Country Music; page 210 © Birthplace of Country Music; page 217 © (top) James Vallee | dreamstime.com; (bottom) Rafael Vilches | dreamstime.com; page 218 © William Wise | dreamstime.com; page 221 © (top left) Jdpphoto12 | dreamstime.com; (top right) Sean Pavone | dreamstime.com; (bottom) Calvin L. Leake | dreamstime.com; page 222 © Calvin L. Leake | dreamstime.com; page 225 © (top) James Becker | dreamstime.com; (bottom) Sandra Burm | dreamstime.com; page 226 © Brandon Upson | dreamstime.com

ACKNOWLEDGMENTS

Writing a travel book in a pandemic is challenging, even if it is one to the place where you live and are quarantining. But for every time I was frustrated, not knowing if or when a museum would reopen, I was grateful for the opportunity to safely explore Middle Tennessee, most often while wearing hiking boots, with my quarantine yellow lab rescue, Raja, in tow.

As always, the thoughtful, smart Leah Gordon helped me sort through it all as only an editor can, helping me look beyond 2020 and to the time that people would be able to explore again. The rest of the Avalon Travel team, including Lucie Ericksen, Darren Alessi, and Megan Anderluh, helped take this new book in a new series from an idea to reality.

Ally Willis was a tenacious photo researcher, tracking down images and permissions in a year when many people were not in their offices.

I'm grateful for the opportunity to share my take on a place that means so much to me with others.

MAP SYMBOLS

═══ Highway	① Thing To Do	▲ Small Park
═══ Primary Road	⊛ National Capital	▲ Mountain Peak
═══ Secondary Road	⊙ State Capital	✦ Unique Natural Feature
── Residential Road	○ City/Town	✦ Unique Hydro Feature
┄┄ Unpaved Road	✈ Airport	⎰ Waterfall
═══ Pedestrian Walkway	✈ Airfield	
---------- Trail		
── Paved Trail		
············· Ferry		

CONVERSION TABLES

$°C = (°F - 32) / 1.8$
$°F = (°C × 1.8) + 32$
1 inch = 2.54 centimeters (cm)
1 foot = 0.304 meters (m)
1 yard = 0.914 meters
1 mile = 1.6093 kilometers (km)
1 km = 0.6214 miles
1 fathom = 1.8288 m
1 chain = 20.1168 m
1 furlong = 201.168 m
1 acre = 0.4047 hectares
1 sq km = 100 hectares
1 sq mile = 2.59 square km
1 ounce = 28.35 grams
1 pound = 0.4536 kilograms
1 short ton = 0.90718 metric ton
1 short ton = 2,000 pounds
1 long ton = 1.016 metric tons
1 long ton = 2,240 pounds
1 metric ton = 1,000 kilograms
1 quart = 0.94635 liters
1 US gallon = 3.7854 liters
1 Imperial gallon = 4.5459 liters
1 nautical mile = 1.852 km

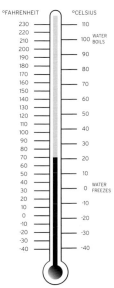

MOON 52 THINGS TO DO IN NASHVILLE

Avalon Travel
Hachette Book Group
1700 Fourth Street
Berkeley, CA 94710, USA
www.moon.com

Editor: Leah Gordon
Acquiring Editor: Megan Anderluh
Series Manager: Kathryn Ettinger
Copy Editor: Sierra Machado
Graphics Coordinators: Lucie Eriksen, Darren Alessi
Production Coordinator: Darren Alessi
Cover Design: Kimi Owens
Interior Design: Darren Alessi
Moon Logo: Tim McGrath
Map Editor: Kat Bennett
Cartographer: John Culp

ISBN-13: 9781640495364

Printing History
1st Edition—January 2022
5 4 3 2 1

Front cover photo: Civil War Fort Negley © Brian Jannsen / Alamy Stock Photo
Back cover photos (clockwise from top): © Anthony Heflin | Dreamstime.com; © Nashville Paddle Co.; © Paweł Gubernat | Dreamstime.com; © Asakalaskas | Dreamstime.com; © Brent Hofacker | Shutterstock.com

Printed in Malaysia for Imago